A Step Outside

Understanding the nature, history, and
philosophy of the land around us

Michael Faherty

ISBN: 978-0-578-80287-9 (Print)
ISBN: 978-0-578-80288-6 (Ebook)

Cover Illustration by Matthew Faherty

Dedicated to my wife Jennifer,
and my children, Isabel, Matthew, and Sophia.

Contents

Essais

Preface

Every truthful study of near and simple objects will
qualify you for the more difficult and complex.
—Asher Durand

Thank you for opening this book and for indulging my attempt to write on a series of topics about landscape and nature. Herein you will find 52 short pieces written weekly from July 2019 to June 2020. In homage to the questing mind and the generous prose of the Renaissance French humanist Michel de Montaigne, I call the entries "Essais," seeking to capture the original sense of the word as literary exploration and exposition. Just as with Montaigne's *Essais*, this book is not meant to be read continuously from beginning to end, but rather, if at all, in small pieces based on your preference.

As you will see, I delve into a variety of themes—historical, literary, philosophical, architectural, topological, and lexicographical. I avoided cutting down the writing and have left all 52 essais nearly as originally written to reflect my sometimes jagged, but always well-meaning course of thought. We live our lives in short daily and weekly chunks, and these essais capture a mind's inquiry over the bumpy path of time.

For a long while, I have had an interest in the experience of the land—walking through wilderness, farmlands, suburbs, or cities—with curiosity about the surrounding environment. Geology, topography, hills, fields, woods, homes, parks, commercial buildings, paths, and roads all provide fascination.

I seek to understand the history and legacy of our surroundings, natural and human-made, evolving through time. What are the elements of the landscape around us? How did it become this way? How has it changed? Seeing an old building or a rocky outcrop strikes a subliminal chord in me, and in these essais, first and foremost, I wanted to share and explain their resonance.

And then there are more substantial issues. In my studies, I found a fundamental division between ourselves and the world around us. Humans and nature have become separate. The land around us is developed and exploited for our use. For the most part, we are oblivious to our effect on the world. As we denature the land and extract resources from it, we seem intent on making our world environmentally and aesthetically destitute. Even worse, as individuals, we've become intellectually, emotionally, and spiritually more impoverished due to this separation. There is a despondency to the modernism of our lives, which I believe is due largely to the wedge between us and the potential goodness of nature and the land.

Woven through these essays is a surreptitious call to action. My wish is to incite awareness and spark curiosity about the origins and history of our natural and human-made landscapes. I hope to instill an imperative for us to go out and reconnect with our surroundings, with the goal of a deeper connection to the world around us and our evolving selves. The act of going out onto the land can be one of transcendence, moving our spirits beyond the egoic to the immanent. The philosopher Lao Tze wrote, "A sage dwells within all beneath heaven at ease, mind mingled through it all." I hope for an uplifting of the mind, a broadening of knowledge about the land, and a change in how we think about and treat nature.

Michael Faherty
Ridgewood, New Jersey
October 2020

ESSAI 1
What Happened?

The mass of men lead lives of quiet desperation.
—Henry David Thoreau.

What happened to your life? So much of it is spent inside, indoors with your head tilted down, typing away on your cell phone, computer, or tablet. Sometimes your head tilts upwards to look at the TV across the room that is inexplicably turned on despite the fact that you have several other devices already on. We have trained our neck muscles to look up and look down, up again and then down again, but rarely do we swivel our view from side to side.

Do you ever get a feeling of simultaneous stress and lethargy, a wave of physical ennui that washes over you from over-surfing those texts and tweets and posts and articles for too long? It is that tension you feel when you know you are wasting your time thumbing away at your personal device, addictively and unconsciously consuming zero-value information. It is the tiredness in your limbs from sitting too long, not moving, while your eyes strain to peer at the small screen, and the headache grows behind your left temple.

You know what you are doing is not suitable for you. Your dog walks over and gives you the come hither look, asking to go outside. Maybe she senses that you are the one that needs to

1

be taken for a walk. You sit there and sense the headache and turn away from the dog and go back to the phone or tablet or laptop as you focus on that tweet about that star who is dating that other star.

Or maybe the feeling is that malaise that washes over you as you sit in the three-hour meeting in the soulless gray conference room while the presenter drones through 127 PowerPoint slides. You know that feeling that you would rather be anywhere else? You look to distract yourself by glancing at your computer, and you see a new email about a production problem, or an accounting mistake, or a consumer complaint, or a people issue, or a new company process—and your gut clenches a bit. Unthinkingly, you start typing a response to the email, and your sense of the world narrows to this one minor issue. Your eyes and brain focus on the screen, and the rest of life fades. Unnoticed are the leaves on the trees outside the window of the gray-walled conference room. The leaves flutter in the breeze, dappling the grass below with light and shadow. You are oblivious, and 15 minutes of your precious life go by as you type and type and type. Maybe, just maybe, you look up and gaze out the window and see the tree and the leaves and the light. You suddenly wonder what it would be like to be a tree, just standing there with your feet on the ground and limbs reaching up to the sky. How simple life would be! And then your coworker next to you gives you a nudge.

Later on, after consuming way too much food at dinner — too much bread or spaghetti or French fries or beer — you sit on the couch with a remote control in your right hand and four cream-filled cookies in your left, and you watch all of these these people doing cool things on the TV screen. Click the remote, and you see young chefs with mind-boggling culinary skills whipping together multi-course meals in competition with famous judges. Click again, and you see detectives solving crimes through analysis and action, all while being part of a close team of experts and friends working in sync to uphold justice and protect the citizenry. Click the remote once more, and there is that reality TV show where the contestants compete on a tropical island or in treks and races around the world, pushing their physical and mental limits and proving to themselves how much they can do. Somehow the self-actualization of others has become your entertainment. It is like you are at the bottom of a mountain watching the people on television hiking, almost sprinting, up the slope in front of you towards new and better things. Meanwhile, you are motionless at the bottom of the hill with that remote control and those cookies, which you eat mindlessly one at a time.

What is going on here? It hasn't always been like this. When you were young, you played games outdoors with your friends and went on hikes and had adventures. You learned new things. As a kid, you did some homework with real paper and pencils at a wooden desk. You read actual books with pages. You biked into town and met up with your friends. You were active and skinny, flexible and fast—at least more active, skinnier, more flexible, and faster than you are now. You helped out around the house or the yard, but mostly you did what you wanted to do. You biked and you ran, or kicked around a ball, or played hide and seek. And when you were a teen, and maybe even in your 20s, you worked harder, but there was still such a sense of possibility—a feeling of life's potential mixed in with the randomness of friendships, first jobs, hobbies and sports. You went to the beach. You swung at baseballs and softballs or caught footballs and Frisbees. You met up with folks in the neighborhood. You were out and around. Life was more vibrant and more savory then because it was newer and fresher. Although you would never say your life is now rotten or moldy or old, life maybe feels kind of over-ripe and a bit stale, perhaps having reached its "best when used by" date. Perhaps it is time to clean out your fridge?

Do you feel that life has become less random and less filled with potential? I know I have felt that way. I have been that person vegged out in front of the TV, that person mentally stuck in the conference room, and that person furiously texting while real life happens around me. I've been down and depressed. I've had chunks of past years where I've been mentally mired in stress from work or from family. I've wondered whether I made poor choices in my career, playing the 'what if' game—what if I just waited for that other assignment, what if I had left the company and tried being an entrepreneur, what if I had only worked harder or smarter all of these years. While I have had good jobs and while my family has been a blessing, I found I could not summon up gratitude and happiness for my good fortune. The future seemed just like more of the same—more days at work, more weekends frittered away driving to the mall or feet up in front of the TV, more errands, and more things to do—but all with less time left. Life was passing by, incomplete, misdirected, and a bit bereft.

So what did I do? Well, I read many books about success, goals, happiness, and grit. I learned how to plan my day, how to "live each day to the fullest!" and how to be grateful for the simple things. I spoke to coaches and mentors. I talked with friends and family. All of the advice I got was good, but in the end every self-help thing I tried was just really a Band-Aid over a chronic wound. Trying to reframe my experiences and memories and spin them more positively felt like rearranging the deck chairs on the Titanic. Those chairs were comfortable, but the ship was still sinking. I needed psychic healing and spiritual sustenance, but knowledge was only getting me so far. I required inspiration, but even more importantly, I needed to take a different path.

One morning, a bit overcome by the stress of the upcoming day, and not wanting to exercise or read or do emails, I decided I would simply go outside and wander around a bit. And I did just that. I put on my blue nylon Adidas jacket and my beige hiking shoes and took a walk. I only went out for 15 minutes, and I did not even leave my neighborhood, but I found that the walk helped. I'm not sure what it actually did for me. I felt happier during the walk and more settled afterward. My work that day seemed a bit easier, and I found I connected more with the people around me.

So without setting any specific goals, I simply started to head outdoors more and to look for opportunities to explore. I did not do it every day, but I looked for times for myself in the morning, at lunch, or in the evening when I could head outside. I also headed out on weekends or on vacations to places that seemed fun or exciting—a trail in a nearby park, a neighborhood with older homes, a town center with shops and people. I found that heading outside was a bit about the exercise and fresh air, but even more about where I was and what I was seeing. The landscape around me ignited my curiosity. Why is this town park designed with geometrically laid out paths while this other park has curving garden walks? What style are these square, three-story old houses in this neighborhood, and when were they built? Where does that stream go when it heads into that culvert?

I also began to reflect on the things I had enjoyed most when I was younger. For example, when I was a kid, I always loved maps. I have two brothers and three sisters, and we are all close in age, but on long family car trips, I was always the one who handled the big Esso fold-out Eastern United States highway map. I would trace my finger along our route and call out distances to my dad up front. That big map gave me the big picture of how geography fits together, the proximity of different cities, and the contours of the land—mountains, rivers, bays, and oceans.

As a teen, I read the fantasy classic, *The Lord of the Rings*. I fell in love with JRR Tolkien's epic and his detailed maps and descriptions of the landscape of Middle-earth. Part of my fascination came from how Tolkien linked heroic characters and their inherent goodness to a closeness to nature and the land. In fact, landscape was almost an added character throughout the books.

Later, in college and then in graduate school, without being fully aware of why, I enrolled in and did well in courses on landscape history and landscape architecture. For both my undergraduate and graduate schools, I chose universities famed for their historical campuses. I simply loved walking alongside old buildings and through quads. At the University of Virginia, a friend of mine and I would road-trip up to Monticello, Thomas Jefferson's estate on a mountain nearby, just to hang out and walk around. After that, in my 20s, I lived in New York City and developed a fascination with Central Park. I not only dug into the park's history and the genesis of its design but I also intentionally explored the park—routing my daily walk to the office across the park, tracing the old horse trails, noting the rare, historic elms.

I quickly understood that beyond the simple benefits of being outdoors, the notion of landscape and exploring with curiosity re-engaged a part of me that had been dormant. My hope with these essays is to similarly re-awaken you to nature, to the land, to the built landscape, and most importantly, to your true self. My goal is to inspire you to break free physically and mentally from past habits of mind and body and start something new. Throughout, I will try to instill curiosity regarding words and places and design and people. Undergirding it all is a belief that change in one's life is determined by the actions one takes and what one sees and learns through those actions. The first and most important action is the one you do by yourself and for yourself—the preparation for your other life experiences. Walking outdoors through the landscape can prepare the mind and body for those life experiences and make them better.

In the end, the experience of the natural and man-made world is personal and specific to your desires, your needs, and your approach. Whether it is as simple as opening your eyes a bit more during the daily dog walk, or whether you begin to venture on longer journeys or travel to specific destinations, the hope is that these weekly writings will offer a path or a trail forward for you. What you find at the end of your journey could be your best new self.

ESSAI 2
Outside

I love the picturesque glitter of a summer's morning's landscape. It kindles this burning admiration of nature and enthusiasm of mind.
—*Ralph Waldo Emerson*

So what is it about going outdoors, walking in nature, and observing the landscape? Why should we do it? Are there physical benefits? Are there psychological benefits? Are there spiritual benefits? (Yes to all three!)

We know we are often happier when we are out wandering around walking, but let's delve a bit into what I would call the philosophical mechanism behind landscape enjoyment. We need to go back a bit in history to understand how others first captured the deeper meaning found in the outdoor experience.

First, let's acknowledge that our past is full of scientists, philosophers, poets, writers, and politicians who actively pursued strolling, walking, hiking, or venturing as part of their desire to connect with the world and to stimulate their creative selves. When we learn of and read the works of the English poet William Wordsworth, or the French philosopher Jean Jacques Rousseau, Albert Einstein, Charles Dickens, Friedrich Nietzsche, John Quincy Adams, or Harry Truman, we find that a significant part of their days and lives involved solitary journeying outdoors. They saw their walks and hikes as recuperative—an emotional and intellectual trigger for their endeavors. The English poet William Wordsworth wrote: "Come forth into the light of things. Let Nature be your teacher." His most famous poems sought to capture the magic of the landscape observed, embodied, and imbued: "How does the meadow flower its bloom unfold? Because the little flower is free down to its root, and, in that freedom, bold."

Wordsworth's theme of nature linked to the ideas of freedom, humanity, and immanence that typify the Romantic period, which stretched from the late 18th century to the mid-19th century. Romantic poets and philosophers exemplified and explained the connection between the artist and the landscape, venturing out into the world and then playing back what they saw in their works. It is in the writings of this period where we can best understand what we often feel and experience in walking the landscape.

Romanticism in the United States manifested most notably in the Transcendental movement of the 1840s and 1850s in New England. At that time, New England was on the verge of industrialization with communication networks (canals, railroads, roads) netting the land and factories emerging in cities and towns. The countryside was in between an agrarian, small-town past, and an industrial, urban/suburban future. Transcendentalists sought the direct experience of nature, searching for a pre-modern truth about humankind's place in the world.

The leading Transcendental writer and lecturer was Ralph Waldo Emerson. For Emerson and his cohort, the individual and, specifically, the soul of the individual matters most. Life is not just about facts and rationality; it is not just about science and industry or logic. Understanding the world relies equally on the subjective consciousness of the individual. We both seek to understand the world and then interpret that world for ourselves and others. Value comes through observation and letting our soul touch on and reflect the facts we see. Experience is, therefore, elevated from the mundane to be more spiritual and inspiring.

In his 1836 essay, "Nature," Emerson captures the importance of getting oneself outdoors to reconnect with life and rebuild the soul. For Emerson, a walk through the landscape relieved the tyranny of the mundane: "To the body and mind which have been cramped by noxious work or company, nature is medicinal and restores their tone." In Emerson's view, walking through nature is a tonic for the soul which restores equilibrium. The duality and separateness of ego and the larger world disappears. Soul and nature reacquire their original one-ness: "Standing on the bare ground—my head bathed by the blithe air, and uplifted into infinite space,—all mean egotism vanishes. I become a transparent eye-ball." For Emerson, experience needed to be direct, in the moment, and tactile to be spiritual and soulful.

In my life, I find that merely heading outside for a walk or a bike ride creates a mental break—a stoppage of the inexorable chatter and commentary in my head. My inner voice—always planning, often rehashing—masks contact with the present moment and the sense of the real me, my true nature, and my soul. For me, the bracing sublime of natural forms — sky, hills, streams, woods, and fields — interlaced with our human-made world fascinates and stimulates. In nature, I see the reality of the world as it is both in the present moment and persisting through time. The duality of me versus the world lessens and even sometimes disappears.

In my first steps out into the street, I always have to commit myself to "noticing" -- to looking around. I have to intentionally, and with extra effort, steer my awareness away from the mental chatter—the worrying and the stress, the revisiting of the past and the planning for the future, the absurd and never-ending dialectic of the stream of thoughts in my head. I must return my mind to the present moment to truly encounter my surroundings. My intent as I walk must be explicit: to notice the details of the landscape and to start questioning the why, the purpose behind the design I see.

For example, I may see a house. And then my mind registers that the house is a Victorian. And then I see that it has a barn in back. And then I see that the barn seems older than the house and is of an older design. And then I think the Victorian might not be the original home on the lot, and I wonder what made this lot so unique that a home from maybe the Federal era might have been here originally.

Maybe then I see a brook cutting underneath the street. I try to discover the source of the brook, which may be a natural spring. I try to surmise where the stream goes — what river does it flow into? And then, as I trek alongside the stream, I see remnants of an old mill dam. I try to make out the contours of where the old mill pond stood.

And perhaps then I turn to hike up a hill, and I wonder about the hill's geology. Why do the ridges in my town run from the northeast to the southwest? What are all of these boulders scattered around? Why are the older houses all made of the same stone? And isn't it surprising (or not) that the stone in the homes matches the stone girding the brook nearby?

Step by step, each "why?" question leads to other, deeper thoughts. We make linkages and form hypotheses. I walk with purpose but allow myself to turn and explore at random. Eventually, I return home wanting to learn more, primed to research some new facts. I am physically charged and intellectually activated. I sense an inchoate meaning about the world I inhabit and my place in it. I have a forward sense of momentum for the remainder of the day and an overarching sense of balance and perspective. I've bolstered a more genuine sense of self.

Next time you are out, stand still with your eyes shut and just breathe and listen. Hear the sounds of nature, the leaves, the birds, the breeze, or the rain. Catch the noises of cars or trains or planes. The noise surrounds you while you remain still. You can feel a separateness between you, the listener, and all of the noises that you hear. Now, imagine that your brain and your body are no longer separate but one thing all together. Thinking of yourself as connected to the world in this way lets you capture the feeling of transcendence. As Emerson writes, "Nature is made to conspire with spirit to emancipate us." It certainly can.

ESSAI 3
Awesome

*The glacier was God's great plough set at work ages
ago to grind, furrow, and knead over, as it were,
the surface of the earth.*

—*Louis Agassiz*

Here's is an idea that should awe us! Twenty thousand years ago
in the northern third of the United States, there were no people,
no trees, no animals, no civilization, no land, just icy desolation
entombing the ground where many of us now live. Giant sheets
of ice extended down from the North Pole, covering the places
where our cities and suburbs and farms and shopping malls
now lie. Massachusetts, Connecticut, Rhode Island, Vermont,
New Hampshire, and Maine were all one big ice cube. A mile
of ice topped Manhattan and northern New Jersey. The top
third of Pennsylvania, Michigan, Minnesota, and Wisconsin
were all frozen too. Today's map of the upper Midwest, upstate
New York, and Canada is replete with lakes small and large,
evidence of this significant, peculiar, icy/watery event. The
Great Lakes themselves are a huge remnant of something that
was inconceivable and unexplainable for a long time.

That long unexplained phenomenon, we now know, is
the Laurentide ice sheet, named for the Laurentian mountain
chain in southern Quebec. The Laurentide was a giant,

continent-covering glacier that flowed over Canada and the top third of the Midwest and Northeast United States from 90,000 years ago until its retreat about 15,000 years ago. At its peak, the Laurentide was a land crushing and carving icecap on the earth, and, as it receded, it left vast tracts of water, many of which we still see today in our maps and local landscapes.

From whence did this giant glacier come? A glacier is a flowing mass of ice that originates from one of two sources. During the ice ages, ancient glaciers emerged in the Arctic or Antarctic polar climates of the high latitudes and flowed down across the land. Greenland and Antarctica are landmasses still covered with glaciers, although less so recently due to global warming. Glaciers also can be found on mountaintops and in mountain valleys at high elevations. If you've seen images of Mount Everest, downward flowing glaciers cover large parts of the mountainside.

Snowfall compacting over time into deeper and deeper masses creates glacial ice. The ice's weight causes friction with the land underneath, resulting in a sheen of water between the glacier and the underlying rock or soil. This watery barrier enables the ice to move, or flow over the land as it is pulled by gravity. As the glacier flows, it picks up dirt, sand, and rocks, sometimes carving huge chunks of rock from mountainsides or from ridges and other times bulldozing soil or rock and creating valleys. If the valleys are close to the ocean, seawater will backfill the valleys when the ice melts, creating fjords. Rivers also flow under glaciers, shifting sand and gravel towards lower elevations and the forward edge of the ice.

The most recent glacial interlude, the Laurentide, was the culmination of the Pleistocene Epoch, which lasted from 2.6 million years ago to 13,000 BCE and featured a series of recurring global ice events. "Pleistocene" comes from Greek, meaning "most new." When we were kids, we learned that we lived in the Pleistocene Epoch and that we reside on earth during a brief interlude between ice ages. This is no longer deemed true. There is agreement in the science community that due to global warming and the impact of humans and their technology on the earth, we are now in a newly-labeled epoch, the "Holocene," meaning "entirely recent." Humans have disrupted a 2.6 million year ice age cycle (hmmm...hurray for us?).

The ice ages are over (we think), but we still see the detritus and land-shaping evidence of those enormous ice floes without too much trouble. The time since the last ice sheet receded in North America is a blink of the eye in the geologic time scale. The Atlantic Ocean is 130 million years old. Dinosaurs went extinct sixty-five-million years ago. The last ice age was just a few thousand years in the past, a few hundred genera-tions of man. The remaining lakes of upper North America are the most visible trace of the recent presence of the glaciers, but there are others. Glaciers pushed rock, dirt, and sand at their forward edges. At a glacier's furthest extent, soil and rock accumulated and remained as hills as the glaciers began to recede. These hills and mounds are called "moraine," and the line of the moraine from the latest glacial advance tracks across the Midwest, Pennsylvania, New Jersey, Staten Island, Long Island, and Cape Cod. The same Laurentide ice sheet that created the morainal hills near Greensburg, Indiana deposited the island of Nantucket off of Massachusetts.

I grew up and lived most of my life at the margin of the once-extensive Laurentide ice. I was born on Long Island, a ninety-mile pile of glacial moraines and outwash plain that stretches out 90 miles east from Manhattan. I used to look out my bedroom window as a boy from my Long Island home, which was located on an actual moraine hill. At night I could look out onto a glacial outwash plain (the sandy, flat areas created by the flow of water from the melting glacier) now covered with lights of roads and stores and suburbia. In my 20s and 30s, I lived in New York City and southern Connecticut, where I could observe the kettle ponds (left by chunks of glacial ice that melted into permanent ponds), and the north/south striations on the exposed bedrock from stones dragged by the ice sheet to and fro. I proposed to my wife at Montauk Point, at the far end of Long Island, in the lee of an eroded moraine cliff of rocks, sand, and dirt.

Glacial moraines have a peculiar topography. They are rows of hills rising above the surrounding countryside, providing the northern border for the flat outwash plain where the water from the glaciers carried sand and gravel from the melting ice. Morainal land is uneven with swales and mounds, which are perfect for golf courses as they replicate the landscape of Scotland, itself a post-glacial countryside where the sport originated. On Long Island, the Bethpage Black and Shinnecock Hills golf courses are both built on glacial moraines and, every few years, one or the other serves as a venue for the US Open or PGA Championship tournament.

When the glaciers were melting, the moraines often held back the meltwater for a period of time, creating glacial lakes. In northern New Jersey, near where I live now, meltwater formed two lakes, Paramus and Passaic, and one can still see the remnants of these lakes today as lower marshy lands which now house shopping malls and highways. Kettle ponds can be found scattered across the countryside of New England and the upper Midwest. The Finger Lakes in upstate New York come from meltwater, as well as the five Great Lakes.

In addition to the moraine hills and glacial ponds, there are other landforms created by retreating ice including kames, which are small hills formed by ice melt dropping layers of soil over time; eskers, which are twisty hills created by streams under the glacier that deposited sediment; and drumlins, which are long hills left by retreating ice. Morainal mounds exist at the terminus of the glacier (terminal moraines) or where a glacier may have paused or expanded intermittently during the melting period.

Other glacial evidence includes erratics, which are rocks or even huge boulders transported by the ice and dropped tens of miles from their source. A mile from my home is a giant glacial erratic, the "Glen Rock," an eponym for the town where it resides. Another local erratic called the "Atlas Stone" sits atop the New Jersey Palisades, the cliffs that line the New Jersey side of the Hudson River across from Manhattan. This rock weighs fifteen tons and is arched underneath. On the bedrock below the big stone one can view the scratches from other stones dragged by the Laurentide glacier. For 19th century geologists, these striations (and the presence of the Atlas rock itself) provided proof that glaciers topped the Palisades and indeed covered all of New York City.

So what is the purpose of all of this knowledge of the Ice Age? The Ice Age's remarkable evidence surrounds many of us and defines the landscape on which many of us live. It is geology that is near contemporaneous to our times. The contemplation of the undergirding substance and history of our landscapes deepens our connection to the immanence of the world. In seeking to understand the land, we can perhaps gain the humility and joy of having true wonder and awe.

ESSAI 4
Landscape

*We are still in Eden; the wall that shuts us out of
the garden is our ignorance and folly*

—*Thomas Cole*

New York's Metropolitan Museum of Art houses arguably the
most famous landscape painting in American history. Head
into the museum on 5th Avenue, climb up the main staircase
to the second floor, and make your way to the American wing
towards the back and to the right. There you will find "The
Oxbow" by Thomas Cole.

Pause now, study the painting, and take it in. Cole painted
a view of the 270-degree oxbow bend in the Connecticut River
near Northhampton, Massachusetts. On the left, we see the
drama of a receding storm and a wild hilltop with jagged trees,
including a small self-portrait of the artist standing at his easel.
The middle and right of the painting captures a broad landscape
of river, fields, and farmhouses. It is a landscape in transition
and in motion, with trees being cut down, smoke coming from
forests, clouds moving out, and sunlight beaming in. We see the
juxtaposition of natural elements and human-made landscape.
We understand the evolution of the land below us, elided into
a snapshot, a moment of perspective and view.

Many aspects of the scene are unremarkable—the typical

tilled fields, the artist's comical hat—yet there is a more significant presence at hand with the brightly lit sky on the right overcoming the storm clouds as they recede. That light, revealing the bend in the river and shining down on the farms, feels otherworldly, message-borne, and perhaps redemptive. We search the landscape, curiously looking for clues to understanding, while also reveling in the sublime whole. We see a panorama of nature and man, and man's impact on nature. And we are part of the landscape in that we define it by viewing it. Just like the artist, our perspective and interpretation influence the aesthetics of the painting.

The 1933 edition of the *Oxford English Dictionary*, volume VI, page 53 defines "landscape" in the first instance as "a picture representing natural inland scenery," and, secondly, as "a view or prospect of natural inland scenery, such as can be taken in at a glance from one point of view." Both definitions capture this idea of a scene: what we see in the instant from the eyes out to a singular prospect. Landscape is the land and the elements of the earth—geological contours and features, flora, fauna, structures—that we view in one sweep of our gaze. When we think of landscape paintings like "The Oxbow" this is what we see in them: mountains, forests, fields, houses, paths, buildings, roads, people, and animals.

Harvard historian John Stilgoe writes, "…landscapes display a fragile equilibrium between natural and human force" (*Common Landscape of America, 1580 to 1845*.) Landscape is not just the natural world; it is the natural world as it's impacted, lived in, designed, altered, maintained, and most importantly viewed by people. Landscape is not just nature, even though it is filled with natural elements. Landscape is undoubtedly not wilderness, although it initially emerged from the wilderness. Landscape is triply dynamic—it's an ongoing echo of original nature delineated and designed and redesigned by people, and then seen by you. As such, landscape communicates culture and heritage, community, and belief. Landscape is an intimate history that tells us about our past and invites questions. We want to seek deeper and deeper connection to the landscape around us and our place in it.

Another, older use of the word "landscape" was as a compendium or a summary of a larger work. What we see when we view landscape is static in the moment, just a caesura in what is a long story that has evolved through natural and human-made impact. I recently stood on a rocky outcrop, atop a high ridge near where I live in New Jersey. I stood staring out east over a wide valley—15 miles of developed countryside with the buildings of Manhattan in the distance. As with the Thomas Cole painting, I could itemize the details of the land below: Highway 208, the Nabisco Factory, the false belfry atop Ridgewood high school, the office complex, the town pool, the grid of streets, the clouds above, and scattered planes heading towards Newark Airport. But what I was really seeing was the accumulation of the effect of man over time. The outcrop on which I stood was comprised of basalt cooled from a series of prehistoric volcanic eruptions. Sandstone from a prior inland sea limned the valley below. The buildings in the vale ranged in age from 250 years to 25 days old. The landscape had persisted and evolved through time, and what I was viewing was a summation of various natural and human-made impacts.

While my view was perhaps less dramatic than the Thomas Cole painting, I still felt the same sense of static moment reflecting ongoing dynamism. Just as we move through our lives, landscapes evolve through time. We get a glimpse of it as we look out, but it will be different tomorrow and, in fact, be changed even in the next moment. We, too, will be changed, and it is this ever-changing juxtaposition of the viewer and viewed that can create a feeling of wonder in ourselves and the world around us.

So what is required of us? Well, landscape requires us to take action. The verb "to land" connotes the idea of alighting onto the land: the boat landed on shore; the plane landed on the runway; the Apollo 11 lunar module landed on the moon. Land is an object, a thing upon which we must step out onto. This requires an exiting or departure from where we are, out of the structure that encases us. We must make an "escape" from our current place (inside of something) to a new location (the land outdoors). We escape onto the land to become immersed in landscape. We are vital and forceful and moving. We execute a "land escape." We go outside to experience the world.

ESSAI 5
Great Heart

"Wheresoever you go, go with all your heart."
—*Confucius*

When I was younger, I bought into the running craze that began back in the 1970s. Back then, it was all about the headbands and those super short shorts that showed off way too much leg. You still see folks running on the sidewalks or in the streets today, but they are now garbed in spandex and high-tech shirts that wick the sweat away from the body. I look at the faces of these folks running, and I do not sense a great deal of fun. What I see is pain. The visage of a runner carries at best a tight-lipped grimace, but often a look of slack-jawed, wide-eyed desperation.

There is a reason for this. We now know that running long distances as a primary form of exercise is simply bad. Don't do it! Beyond the stress it puts on your knees, feet, and back, running neither burns a significant amount of fat nor does it build much muscle. A fast-paced walk will get your heart rate up to about 60 to 70% of its max (max=the heart rate during extreme aerobic exercise). For me, 65% of max is about 115 heartbeats per minute, and I can get to this rate if I am striding with purpose with a bit of arm swing, a bit slower on the uphills, and a bit faster on the downhills. I know I am in the zone when I feel a slight bit of sweat, but my breathing is still not labored.

Your friendly cardiologist* will tell you that simply getting your heart rate up to this reasonable level, targeting 65% of your max heart rate, exercises your heart and burns off fat. It is the zone that is best suited for weight loss. At any lower rate than this, your heart will not be pumping enough, and the fat will not burn. Any faster and your body shifts to an anaerobic mode and starts burning the sugar out of your blood, which creates lactic acid in your muscles leading to soreness the next day. It is almost as if some human designer is telling us, "Go out and take a good walk, and great things will happen, but don't overdo it!"

We are designed for distance. Hominids—the primate family that includes us modern-day humans and our evolutionary predecessors—have two traits which enable our walking power. The first is bipedalism. Quite simply, humans walk upright on two legs (bi-pedal) while most other animals do not. It is not known for certain why early humans developed the trait. Darwin thought that the feature evolved to free up the hands to carry and use tools. Some anthropologists believe it was due to the elimination of forest two million years ago and the need for early hominids to see prey or danger further, across fields, from a higher vantage. The ability to rise up and see the world around us differentiates us from so many of our animal friends. My little golden retriever's point of view is from 18 inches off the ground, and most of her outside experience is with her nose down, scanning just 20 or 30 yards around.

A second evolved trait is our ability to walk (or hike, jog, run) for more extended periods than other animals. Our legs cover more distance per stride than our ape cousins. Our relative lack of body hair and proliferation of sweat glands create a fantastic cooling system to avoid overheating from exertion. Our ability to leverage different types of nutrition that allow for efficient energy utilization fuels sustained efforts. Our bodies are perfected to move across the landscape. Early humans developed these traits because of the benefit they gave in persistence hunting, where an animal is wounded or driven to exhaustion over long distances. Humans cannot out-sprint their prey, but they can outlast their prey, wearing them down over time.

We are designed to move across the land. We are designed to look around at the land and see things. Yet, we have developed a world that limits our naturally designed traits. Sitting in the conference room and trolling through Twitter are antithetical to our nature. We must go out and move around. The goal here is to get the blood pumping through your body, so the muscles awaken. And it is not just the leg muscles that perk up on a walk; you will be surprised at how your shoulders and abdominals are involved. The other thing I love with aerobic exercise is how the blood pumps out to the skin. In winter, your skin will flush as the blood is pumped, working to warm your outer layer. In the warmer months, you'll develop a sheen of sweat, but that's okay because it is a signal something good is happening (remember, breathing hard or sweating too much means you are going too fast!).

When I am moving along with pace, I get the feeling like I am accomplishing something. I feel invigorated and no longer wrapped up in my inner monologue. My goal is to feel "great-hearted" in the sense that in my walking, my heart is beating powerfully to its true purpose. When walking or bike riding, I feel enabled to do things I otherwise could not do.

In John Bunyan's 1678 allegory *Pilgrim's Progress*, his character "Greatheart" has the physical and moral strength to help the heroine Christiana on her journey. He is great-hearted in both body and spirit. This is why we exercise the heart—for physical strength and subsequent spiritual strength. We want our hearts to burst with joy and love and guide us to do great things, to help others. This is our goal when walking—to become great-hearts!

PUBLIC SERVICE ANNOUNCEMENT!: always check with your doctor before starting any exercise routine, even walking.

ESSAI 6
Freedom

Freedom is nothing but a chance to be better.
—Albert Camus

In the United States, we talk of freedom as a core value that is intrinsic to who we are or what we hope to be. Thomas Jefferson defined freedom for Americans in the Declaration of Independence as "life, liberty, and the pursuit of happiness." We were intended to be alive, to be free, and to find happiness. Abraham Lincoln talked of the Civil War as initiating a "new birth of freedom," expanding liberty for all the country's people.

Yet, are we free? The poet Robert Browning writes, "So free we seem, so fettered fast we are!" While we talk of freedom, our obligations and environment often confine us. Social or work requirements often demand that we awaken at a specific time, dress a certain way, and head off to pre-planned endeavors. We chose years ago to live in a particular house or apartment, where we now remain because of perhaps the mortgage or the cost of moving elsewhere. Maybe we have kids in school, which further embeds us in a network of local urgencies and errands. The philosopher Soren Kierkegaard, wrote, "Anxiety is the dizziness of freedom." He believed that freedom and the choices that freedom entails create anxiety in us. We are anxious because we have options, and in choosing we know that we will proscribe our own futures and incur the loss of other paths.

Freedom is the exercise of an inherent component of ourselves. It is our ego in action. It is us, self-defined by what we choose to do. Arm and arm with this freedom is the construct of morality, seeking to feel and understand the right choice and then making that choice and acting, with the potential but not the certainty that our right actions freely chosen can lead to happiness. Our lives may feel circumscribed by our past choices, but not always. We can find leeway.

True freedom requires us to have a presence and awareness of ourselves and our activities, to take a bird's-eye view of our lives so we can make choices, versus trundling obliviously forward. The choice to have this awareness is difficult. Self-examination is truth-seeking, and personal analysis is inherently stressful. It requires us to acknowledge that something is wrong, which is not easy. It then requires us to seek solutions to what is wrong, which is difficult. It requires us to decide and act, which is even harder. It demands that we work consistently going forward. It often even asks us to revisit the commitment and question the decision, and whether to continue. Freedom is hard work!

There is a huge benefit, however! With this freedom comes a sense of personal responsibility and concomitant empowerment. Your awareness, your analysis, and your choices are yours. You have taken your liberty into your own hands. You are responsible. Blaming others or blaming circumstances goes out the window. You may exist in a particular context right now, which is a culmination of the choices you have made and the contingent circumstances that have come about, but that time is past. You can now assess and choose for yourself. You can take your freedom upon you.

As we venture out into the landscape, daily or weekly or monthly, we are not looking merely to establish another habit, like "not eating ice cream" or "exercising six days a week." We are looking for walking outside to be a way to establish personal freedom. The choice to walk is the first step—it is our choice to do so or not. The choice of where to walk is also ours. We can imagine ourselves as artists, and the geography we walk across is the canvas. Heading outdoors is the interaction of the free self with the larger world outside, and it is there that our freedom manifests to its greatest extent. That first step outside is breaking free from constraint, and the next steps then warp you into the broader contexts of nature and time. We walk outside to explore and to feel. Our free will seeks solace, or knowledge, or perhaps just surcease. We can walk through the landscape as an essential and transcendent activity. We walk to truly express ourselves, to touch the universal, and to live.

ESSAI 7
Faith, Hope, Charity

So now faith, hope, and love abide, these three;
but the greatest of these is love.

—*Saint Paul*

We have all come across the verbal triptych, "Faith, Hope, and Charity." As a good Catholic boy, I was raised hearing these words and having the sense that they were something I was supposed to have. They are espoused as virtues or ways of being and acting in the world to be a better person. With a bit of research, we also know they were the names of three apocryphal saints: the three daughters of the mother, "Sophia," whose name means wisdom.*

It is no surprise that virtues like charity, hope, and faith emanate from wisdom because enacting them in one's life is wise, no matter your religion. We all need to have some sort of "faith" that there is a construct to the world that makes sense and that our society has meaning. We all must have "hope" that something will happen in the future that is positive for us; otherwise, we despair. And then there is charity, which gives meaning to what we do, as charity is love and love fuels our hopeful intent. The first century AD philosopher Paul of Ephesus (also known as the epistle-writing "Saint Paul") wrote, "And now these three remain: faith, hope and love. But the greatest of these is love." Paul identifies faith, hope, and love as the core virtues, but adds that love of self and others (and if applicable to you, your god) is the most important.

Love is the engine that powers our intent and our actions. When we go out on a walk, we do so because we love ourselves, and walking is a way to care for ourselves physically and emotionally. By taking care of ourselves, we are also taking care of others. As we become a better and stronger person by walking, we are better able to help others through more energy and spirit. "Charity" or love, I think, is the easiest to understand of the three virtues as it is at its core a simple giving of ourselves to others.

Hope is more complicated. Hope is not inherent in our actions the way love is. Hope is something that we have as human beings; it is almost a fact of our humanity. To be human is to hope for something. We can hope for something simple, like warm sunny weather for our hike next Saturday, or for something much grander, like less carbon dioxide emissions for reduced global warming. Hope is something we desire to happen outside our current circumstance that is not totally in our control. Hope is the mind being creative and conjuring, imagining a goal or target made suddenly tangible in our cortex and in our soul. Hope is a harder virtue than love because loving actions often have immediacy, while hope is more about the future and entails uncertainty.

The uncertainty of hope and the resulting anxiety comes about because hope is coupled with doubt. We all doubt whether we have the acumen and gumption to achieve our aims. I can decide I want to walk two miles every morning, but after that goal begins, doubt creeps in. Can I do this? Won't I look silly? The weather is turning colder. I have to get up earlier. What was I thinking? We have doubts and fears, and these creep into our minds. With any hopeful enterprise, we do not have a way of figuring it all out ahead of time. Anything we hope for, especially if it is significant and worthwhile, has a circuitous path to realization, requiring ideas, people, serendipity and circumstance. Hope is illogical because it is founded on a reality that does not yet exist, and doubt seeps into hope's logic gaps and creates cracks in our willpower.

Here is where faith comes in. Faith is the cement that paves over the fissures of doubt. Faith is bravery in the face of setbacks. Faith is the belief that you can still implement your routine despite having to travel for business, despite the small cold you feel coming on, or despite the cold rainy weather. Faith is taking action while ignoring the logic of inaction. Faith is acting "as if" the thing you hope for is going to happen, someway somehow. When we feel that despair in our chests or stomachs at the thought of all we must do this month, this week, or this day, faith is the virtue we summon, which says, "Stop thinking so much, stop telling yourself these mental stories." Just make a to-do list, or if that's too much, get up and make yourself a cup of tea. Faith is doing the things that you know are right with the unproven belief that the future you want in your mind's-eye will result. Faith is self-identity. As we move forward, we are developing our faith in ourselves, and learning to deliver on our hopes, and seeing anxiety and doubt flee.

In the end, 'mother wisdom' is not about an end state, a final accumulation of knowledge, or an achievement of a goal. Wisdom is the process of action, initiated by hope, sustained by faith, and motivated by love. Wisdom is curiosity and exploration. It is the initiative we take to go outdoors and look around and learn and experience the land around us.

Sophia is also the name of my younger daughter.

ESSAI 8
County

O lands! O all so dear to me — what you are, I become part of that, whatever it is.

—Walt Whitman

What is your home turf? What is your stomping ground? On what pasture do you roam? What place do you call home? What is the landscape of your life? Where have you lived the longest, and where do you live now? What is the geography on which most of your life plays out? What is that place that you explore, that you know deeply, and that holds a place in your heart?

We can define our home geographies in many ways. Narrowly but importantly, we can think of the characteristics of our neighborhoods where we walk the dog and chat with the neighbors. There is an intimacy we have with the streets and land close to our home. A bit more broadly, we can reflect on our hometown, where we grew up, or where we now live. Our towns with their schools, shops, parks, and offices have a deep familiarity and often command our highest emotional loyalty. On a larger scale, we all grew up with encouragement to love our state or our nation. We ascribe to the good old U. S. of A. But countries and states are mostly too large to have in-depth knowledge of, defying the intimacy with the land that we aspire to. The regions we hope to know more deeply must include territory broader than that of a neighborhood or town, but still accessible and familiar.

I believe that the county where we live is, in most cases, the right size for our consideration. A shorthand definition of a county might be the land around us that we can manage to visit easily on a given day. A county is a geopolitical entity that is within reach. Back in the 19th century, one could ride a horse across a typical county in a morning and even walk across a county on a long day. A county has a human dimension. It is not too small (we love our hometowns, but they can feel confining) or too big. We can walk or bike ride around our county and discover what is interesting and genuine about it. While seemingly close, neighboring counties have a strangeness to us where we are less sure of the roads or how life happens there. Counties outside of our own are beyond our ken, while our own county has a knowability from accessibility. Often when we are within our home county, we are in our chosen physical and cultural context.

I live in Bergen County, New Jersey, and while I love the place where I live, I sometimes wonder whether there can be any place that sounds less cool, less fun, and less impressive. The name "Bergen" likely refers to a historical hill in the Netherlands (not so romantic), and the state where it resides (New Jersey) isn't quite known for the picturesque. For outsiders, Bergen County may be known firstly as that geographic sprawl of malls where New Yorkers can go to shop and avoid the sales tax. It may also be known as the location of the town of Hackensack, the suburban strawman that Billy Joel mocks in his song "Moving Out." Some may think of Tony Soprano and his heavy accent, or the Joe Piscopo "I'm from Jersey" sketch from Saturday Night Live.

There are undoubtedly many malls in Bergen County, and miles of middle-class homes, drugstores, banks, and high school playing fields. Bergen County often feels like the default setting for the 1950s American dream with all the surface accouterments of a supposed life well-lived. We Bergen folk live in apartments or condos or homes, with our families, pets, and cars. We awaken in the morning to drink some coffee and take the train into the city or drive our vehicles through towns and onto highways to office complexes or local businesses. Weekends include visits to Target or Home Depot in between watching our children play soccer, tennis, or lacrosse.

More people live in Bergen County, New Jersey than live in South Dakota, North Dakota, Alaska, Wyoming, or Vermont. The last census reports 932,000 folks live in Bergen, which perhaps is no surprise. New York City is just a short drive, train ride, or bus trip. Still, this is a lot of people! How can nearly a million people live within 10 miles of my home? It feels overloaded with people, houses, roads, and businesses.

Bergen County is a rectangular chunk of New Jersey, bordered on the east by the Hudson River, on the north by the border with New York State, and on the west by the ridge of the Ramapo Mountains. The southern boundary is irregular, tracing the Watchung Mountain ridge, the Passaic River, and the Hackensack River. Most folks enter the county from the George Washington Bridge, coming over from New York City. The distance from the George Washington Bridge in the southeast corner of Bergen to Bald Mountain at the northwest edge is just 27 miles, which does not feel that big. I live close to the center, and it feels like every spot is reachable, easy to visit.

Dutch and Huguenot farmers initially settled Bergen County in the 17th and 18th centuries. In 1776, George Washington and his troops escaped from the Battle of New York through Bergen County. Bergen was host to the development of early commuter suburbs with the laying of the Erie railroad tracks from Hoboken, Secaucus, and Patterson up through Bergen in several spurs.

The topography of Bergen stems from global tectonic events several hundred million years ago. Bergen County is part of the long Piedmont Plateau, which stretches up and down the East coast of the United States, wedged between the Appalachian Mountains and the coastal flatlands. The Appalachian Mountains rose between 500 and 250 million years ago when an earlier North American proto-continent smashed into an earlier Eurasian proto-continent to create the supercontinent Pangaea. This crashing together created an orogeny, a folding and thrusting upwards of the land. The Appalachians were pushed upwards as a mountain range. The Piedmont formed afterwards, not from a collision of landmasses, but from a later pulling apart of the land when that giant Panagea continent began re-splitting during the Triassic period (250-208 million years ago). This splitting, which re-separated Europe and Africa from the Americas and created the Atlantic Ocean, continues to this day as North America migrates slowly further and further westward. The Piedmont Plateau geology demonstrates the effects of the initial stretching or ripping of the land, as Panagea split in two.

This dynamic geology gives Bergen County a fantastic landscape (and I would argue its attractiveness for the hundreds of thousands of folks who live here). Like much of the rest of the Piedmont plateau, Bergen is underlaid with sandstone and shale derived from past historical epochs as a seabed. This oceanic rock can be seen in the railroad cuts in hillsides throughout the county and in the red stone blocks that the Dutch used for their colonial-era homes. The Ramapo mountain ridge borders the far western edge of the county. As the land stretched in ancient times, this ridge tilted upward on its eastern side as the valley next to it (virtually all of Bergen

County) dropped in elevation, a process called "rifting," which can also be seen today in the Rocky Mountains in Utah and Nevada. The combination of the drop in elevation and the ongoing erosion of the sandstone/shale substrate has made Bergen mostly a large, 20 mile-wide valley.

The rivers of the county flow from the highlands of the west and north southwards to the Passaic River, the Meadowlands, and eventually New York Bay. The erosion from these rivers created an undulating landscape across the county from east to west. Perhaps the county's most dramatic features are the two ranges of basalt hills—the Palisades, which line the Hudson River on the eastern side of the county, and Watchung Mountain, which is further west. As the land pulled apart and stretched thin 200 million years ago, magma surged upward through fissures in the sandstone substrate. The basalt rock that emerged (diabase) was extraordinarily dense and resisted erosion, while the surrounding sandstone deteriorated over time. The result was the emergence of dramatic ridges of volcanic-origin rock, which now yield incredible views of the rolling landscape of Bergen and New York City to the east.

Two of my three children were born in Bergen County. I've lived here with my family and earned my living within its borders for the last 18 years. I am still learning new things each year. I still find glacial erratic boulders, espy old Dutch farmhouses, find 100-year-old trees, and come upon the small downtowns. We take on aspects of the place where we live, becoming part of its evolution and history. Through exploring what is near us, we can develop intimacy with our environs and a sense of caring and ownership. Who we are can be determined by where we are.

ESSAI 9
University of Virginia

*Architecture is my delight, and putting up and
pulling down, one of my favorite amusements.*
— *Thomas Jefferson*

Founded by Thomas Jefferson in 1826, the University of
Virginia represents the culmination of Jefferson's lifetime of
thinking about education, architecture, and landscape. Located
in the foothills of the Blue Ridge mountains in Jefferson's
beloved Albermarle County, the University is considered one
of the top architectural landmarks in the United States and has
been designated a World Heritage site. I was lucky enough to
attend the University back in the 1980s, where I majored in
history and fell in love with the school.

Above my desk, where I am writing now, is a painting of
Jefferson's Rotunda, a half-scale model of the Roman Pantheon,
and the university's architectural focal point. The picture is an
inspiration for me, as it captures in its centerpiece the heroic
historic building as well as the setting of trees and grass that
frame it. By far the largest building in Jefferson's original plan,
the Rotunda, formerly served as a library, and now exists as
a museum and a meeting place for students, professors, and
visitors. Stretching south from the Rotunda is a long grassy
quad, known as "The Lawn." The Lawn is framed on the north

end by the Rotunda with its plaza-like wings. The East and West sides of the quad each feature five "pavilions," or large brick homes. A covered walkway colonnade connects these pavilions onto which student rooms open. Until 1896, the south end of the Lawn was left open with a distant view of the Virginia countryside backed by a spur of hills from the more extensive Blue Ridge mountain range. At the end of the 19th Century, three education buildings (Cabell, Cocke, and Rouse Halls) were built to serve the growing university's needs.*

Each of the ten Pavilions lining the Lawn is unique, highlighting different architectural styles from ancient Greece and Rome, all designed by Jefferson to educate his students in various forms. Each Pavilion also has a two-tiered garden extending behind it, with the garden landscape of each unique and reflecting different styles. Jefferson enclosed each garden with serpentine walls, whose snaking curves allowed efficient construction of only one brick in width. Further out, behind the gardens, parallel to the line of pavilions and student rooms along the Lawn, lie the East and West Ranges consisting of more student rooms and six dining hotels.

Jefferson labeled his design an "Academical Village," and his hope with the interconnecting student rooms, the pavilions designed for professors to live, the gardens, and the central library was to have the educational experience and intellectual intercourse resemble the simplicity and authenticity of a village. Three colors dominate his design—the red of the Albemarle-sourced brick, the white of the classic columns and trim, and the green of the trees and grass. The classical geometry of the architecture superimposed on the rolling greensward of the American Piedmont creates a sublime beauty. Jefferson, in his design for the university, mixed landscape and architectural forms in the service of the aesthetic, and to inspire and inform students. In one sense, the university is very much a classic,

Palladian group of buildings on a hilltop, but it is also set in the midst of gardens and land designs inspired by the English gardening school of the 18th-century.

So how did all of this come to be? How did a plantation owner from the 18th-century American hinterland end up creating what is acknowledged globally as an architectural masterpiece? I chose to go to the University of Virginia in no small part because of the sense of history that permeates the Academical Village today. I continue to appreciate how Jefferson integrated complex forms into such a simple-seeming design. Critically, however, the university's construction was linked with the fact of slave labor in Virginia in the 18th and 19th centuries. Jefferson's vision for education did not include African Americans, and slave labor was essential to his building efforts for both his home, Monticello, and the University of Virginia. Slavery remains a black mark on Jefferson's character and the university's legacy. It is ironic that his words served to support a stratified, racialized society while also evoking a larger sense of liberty that has allowed for the expansion of freedom as time has passed.

Jefferson was a self-educated architect whose library was rife with design books on classical forms. Jefferson explored the classic French formal architecture and gardens when he served as ambassador to France in the 1780s. During that period, he met up with John Adams in England, and they did a self-guided tour of English estate gardens. Jefferson's architectural education manifested first in Virginia with his design of the State Capitol in Richmond. The Capitol is a monumental, columned example of classic design based on an ancient Roman Temple in the south of France. Jefferson's collaboration with Pierre L'Enfant on the original master plan for Washington, D.C., with its unique grid of streets and avenues that radiate from the landmark buildings, reflects the formalism of classic

Michael Faherty

French design that Jefferson saw at Versailles. Jefferson's own home of Monticello, located near the University, was a lifelong architectural project. Monticello demonstrates Jefferson's desire to translate the curvature and more natural-seeming forms of English garden design to his mountaintop home. In all of his projects, Jefferson adopted prior forms to the practical needs of America, whether for a State Capitol building, the layout of streets in a national capital, or his own home.

For Jefferson, translating historic architectural themes was just the starting point. In all of his works, some basic ideas shined through: simplicity and unity of composition; placing classical architecture within the American landscape; the intermingling of informal curved gardens and classic geometry; and siting focal buildings atop hills to be seen while allowing the view of the surrounding land from the architecture itself. The opportunity with the University of Virginia would be to remain true to his lifelong vision while tapping into designs that suited his educational intent.

More than any other early American, Jefferson had a specific educational vision. He wrote in 1810, "no one more sincerely wishes the spread of information among mankind than I do, and none has greater confidence in its effect in supporting good and free government." For Jefferson, education and, specifically, a public educational system was a necessary part of the political revolution in which he participated (and which he led) in the 1770s and 1780s. Jefferson believed "there is a natural aristocracy among men. The grounds of this are virtue and talents...the government is best which provides most effectually for a pure selection of these natural *aristoi* into the offices of government." Jefferson saw an urgent need for government-supported education at a high level to create a merit-based system for future political excellence. As he completed his presidential term in 1808, he envisioned a university that would deliver future generations of leaders for his republic. This would be his life capstone architectural, political, and indeed philosophical project.

To Be Continued

ESSAI 10
Faerie

Come Fairies, take me out of this dull world, for
I would ride with you upon the wind and dance
upon the mountains like a flame!

—*William Butler Yeats*

As a child, I loved fairy tales. I loved fantasy stories like *The Lord of the Rings* and *The Chronicles of Narnia*. The tales were immersive. They provided an escape. There was such a sense of romance in the common boy or girl who, through apparent accident, but really fate, takes on a quest and becomes heroic. Science fiction (which I also love) similarly leverages the idea of quest and heroism, with the setting being a fantastic and different future. Classic novels like Isaac Asimov's *Foundation* series or Robert Heinlein's *The Moon is a Harsh Mistress*, television shows like "Star Trek" or "Battlestar Galactica," and, of course, the "Star Wars" movies, brought us made-up worlds where science was simply a code name for magic. The unexplained power of "dilithium crystals" enabled the Starship Enterprise's warp drive. Luke Skywalker tapped into the mystical, Zen-like "force" to combat foes for freedom and justice in the galaxy. The world was as magical in science fiction as in the medieval romance of the Arthurian legends or Tolkien's Middle-earth.

So let's ponder for a moment the difference between magic

and science. We are all familiar with science as the description of things based on facts rationally thought through. In our world of science, we denote natural phenomena in terms of chemistry and physics. For example, photosynthesis is a chemical process whereby the sun's energy is turned into sustaining fuel for a plant or tree. DNA is the computer-like chemical code that determines the features and traits of all living things. Gravity and the laws of motion predetermine and define the parameters of our physical activity in the world. The afternoon wind I feel walking on the beach is the Coriolis effect—the rush of cool ocean air ocean onto a shore heated by the midday sun. The mass of leaves on the trees that create a green, fluttering wall is nature's way of maximizing the energy-producing surface area of a plant. The ache in my muscles from yesterday's exertions is simply the presence of lactic acid, a byproduct of the use of sugar in my system.

All of this science stuff is true and understandable, but, sometimes, the technicality of the explanations leads to banality. Rational thought sometimes gives me the blahs. I know that the energy that we feel in our bodies is a result of the intake of nutritious foods combined with an exercise plan and proper rest. But vitality in action feels like something more, like an extraordinary power, an imbuing of something beyond rational thought that propels us to go forth and explore. Biologists and behaviorists can certainly describe the feeling of wonder that we feel on seeing a sunrise as the result of an inherited psyche predetermined by evolution to attribute meaning to our external environment. Yet, it seems like there is a more substantial emotion in a sunset that is equally true too. I do wonder whether our rationality gets in the way of our satisfaction.

This may be where magic comes in. We've all heard the word "fey": it is that feeling of otherworldliness and unconventionality that can wash over us at times. The word is linked to the imminence of death, and the freedom from "normal" thought that we adopt when we think of the departure of ourselves or loved ones and embrace thoughts of the eternal. As we contemplate the world beyond ourselves and connect with the sublime, the rational no longer holds sway. We become in touch with magic, both the magic of the world and the magic in ourselves.

In literature, we see this loss of rationality in fairy tales and in fantasy adventures. Works of fiction conjure the world of "Faerie" where physical laws are not absolute. Faerie is the magical world that coexists with our rational world but slightly out of sight and requires particular circumstances to enter. Faerie is a world filled with magically imbued, fantastic flora and fauna and magical beings called fairies. We seek the escape of Faerie because it is a world where the delineation between good and evil is clear. It is a world where we can find ourselves elevated to higher states of consciousness and action.

Finding Faerie is hard. In C.S. Lewis', *The Lion, The Witch, and the Wardrobe*, the children find Narnia through the back of a giant wardrobe and stumble into the world seemingly by accident. In the Harry Potter novels, there is a special entrance to Diagon Alley, the street where magic folk shop for provisions, accessed through The Leaky Cauldron, a pub invisible to the eyes of everyday people. Harry needs at first to be guided to the pub and into the alley by the giant Hagrid. The Leaky Cauldron and Diagon Alley are in London, but not in the London we know.

Similarly, "Platform 9 and 3/4" for the Hogwart's Express train that will take Harry to school is in King's Cross station in London, but is hidden to us muggles (non-magical people) and requires the closing of one's eyes and a leap of faith through a solid wall to get to the new world. The author J.K. Rowling created this alternate magical London that coexists with the real London we all know. To find it, we must have knowledge of it, belief in it, and a faith-like openness to illogic and magic.

And once inside the Faerie world, what is that like? The atmosphere often has a different feel, often denser or heavier, with light being either brighter or dimmer. The passage of time feels different, sometimes stopping altogether. In the universe of J.R.R. Tolkien's *The Lord of the Rings*, the world of Faerie was often signified by entering a forest, often where elves (fairies) lived. The old forest near the Shire housed fairies, like Tom Bombadil and his wife Goldberry. The forests usually felt oppressive and bewildering. One could get lost easily, but they were also magical. In Faerie, trees speak, as do woodland creatures, and these entities usually have accumulated wisdom for those who enter.

The journey into Faerie is initially one of wonder at newness and differentness, followed by a journey to higher wisdom. The world of Faerie challenges the hero to learn, gather new friends and companions, and ultimately win out against the evil in Faerie. The delineation between good and evil is clear, and the hero and the hero's special powers or weapons confront the darkness. But it is the morality, the authenticity of the hero's soul, the bravery, and the hero's self-sacrifice that is the key to conquering the evil emperor or wizard or demon. In Madeleine L'Engle's, *A Wrinkle in Time*, Meg Murray overcomes the evil "It" mind of Central, not through her physical prowess nor any special intelligence, but through her bravery in returning to the planet and by expressing her love for her brother, Charles Wallace. Meg saves her brother, and her family is reunited back on earth. We are left with a tale both of wonder (for example, early in the novel, the old witch Mrs. Whatsit transforming into a flying Pegasus that transports the children through the air across the countryside of the planet they are visiting) and of moral victory.

While us muggles cannot go to distant planets or venture through the back of a wardrobe or leap through a brick wall in King's Cross station, I believe that we can still capture the wonder and morality of Faerie through our experience of the world around us. When we are in the right mood, the world outdoors can become like a faerie land imbued with magic and miracles. We can remain open to the seeming lack of logic in our landscapes. When we are outside trying to calculate the rationality of why this road was built here or why those buildings are situated on the hill over there, we must still remain open to the idea of wonder and indeed magic. Out in the landscape, everything is not entirely in control. Streams carve new paths. Rains create incredibly greenery. Trees and plants spring up in unexpected places. Humans trod unexpected cut-throughs. Owls nest in trees and rabbits burrow into the ground. As individuals, we cannot understand all of the physical and chemical processes underlying the world. For myself I know that I cannot figure everything out. I do not have the time. Nor do I want to burden myself with the need to understand everything. I often just want to experience and not to analyze.

Opening our hearts to the details of the natural landscape can make most everything seem magically and mystically miraculous. The emergence of leaves each spring arrives like a miracle the same week, almost the same day each year. The full moon at night in a crystal sky infuses our bedroom windows with an effervescent shine. When turned loose, my dog runs and leaps with joy for no reason in a supernatural burst of energy. The rationality of environmental science, biology, physics, and chemistry can provide the fact-based rationale behind this phenomena. But the sheer scale of all that is happening around us is awesome in the original sense of the word—we are filled with 'awe.' They say that a butterfly wing flapped in North Africa can create an eventual hurricane in the Caribbean. Sounds logical, but it must be magic, no? The details of the landscape are full of wonder and are wonderful. Although our intellect seeks to fight it, our heart senses the land of faerie around us, filled with awesome, wonderful randomness.

And we want to be in a fairy tale! A fairy tale is an adventure, and an adventure requires a quest to be accomplished and dangers to overcome. We do not shy away from such danger. We do not forsake living the fairy tale. The children in the Narnia series wanted to go on the adventure. Pippin and Merry in *The Lord of the Rings* wanted to go with Frodo to Mordor on the most dangerous adventure of all. The apostles wanted to be with Jesus Christ, despite all of the danger. The football player takes the field, knowing the chance of failure is great and even knowing the eventual injury will come, because it is simply beautiful to be out on the field. Going out into the landscape is a metaphor for something more significant to do with our own lives.

You go into the turbulent outside to have an adventure. At first, the experiences may be small, but then one day, you step off the sidewalk and cut into the woods. You start following the woodland path despite not knowing where it will end. You see new things: that old dam on the brook, the faded red barn, the trail made by kids cutting through to school. You end up in a place where you did not initially plan to go. And all the while, you feel trepidation and anticipation and joy in living for real out in the world.

And you have created a story. You have created your own small fairy story. It could be one in which there is a discovery of new things, or one in which you have faced down danger, or one of pure self-realization, or all of these things. But you have written yourself into a magical story where you are the hero, courageously questing for knowledge and even personal power. The outside is not mundane but dangerous. My one piece of advice is not to be careful! Consider the world of Faerie to be inherent in the world around us. Magic suffuses the landscape. Our job is to be the hero, identifying, contemplating, and acting on our morality as we move through the world.

ESSAI 11
Appalachian Trail

In every walk within nature one receives far more than he seeks.

—John Muir

Much of what interests me concerns discovering the designs and intentions of humans with their landscapes and the benefit of being curious and discovering those intensions. Experiencing and seeing the land and understanding its adaptation to utilitarian and aesthetic needs should be edifying, satisfying, and fulfilling. Our forays across neighborhoods, towns, parks, and cities ignite curiosity around the choices those in the past have made to shape and structure the land.

At times, though, I want to escape from the neighborhood and the sometimes overwrought designs of city or suburb, getting away from all of it to confront a more raw and elemental landscape. One sometimes wants to immerse oneself in pure nature. One wants to test oneself more against the elements; it's a physical but also a mental objective. Can I conquer a trail or a hike or a climb? I get this urge a few times a year, and at least once a year I act on it.

The Appalachian Mountain range extends 1500 miles from Newfoundland and Quebec in Canada down to the north part of Alabama. In the United States, Appalachia includes 14 states and comprises multiple subranges, including the White Mountains in New Hampshire, the Berkshires in Massachusetts and Connecticut, New York's Catskills, the Allegheny range in Pennsylvania, Virginia and West Virginia, the Blue Ridge of Virginia, and North Carolina's Great Smoky Mountains. In colonial days, the range was an initial barrier to westward expansion until later roads and train lines through mountain passes connected east with west. Today, the Appalachians provide a recreational refuge to experience nature, hike, climb, or camp.

The "Appalachian Scenic Trail" traces the ridge of the Appalachian range from Springer Mountain in Georgia up to Mount Katahdin in Maine. A few hundred intrepid hikers each year make the full trek, usually from south to north, over four or five months. I've come across the trail numerous times. In New Hampshire, the trail crosses the Connecticut River near Dartmouth College, where my wife went to school and where we have often visited. I was on the trail when I climbed Massachusett's highest peak, Mount Greylock. When I visited Bear Mountain State Park along the Hudson River just an hour north of New York City, there was the trail again. In New Jersey, at the Delaware Water Gap (where both the Delaware River and Interstate 80 cuts through the Kittatinny Ridge in a deep gorge), the trail popped up again. In Pennsylvania, the trail runs along South Mountain near the Gettysburg Battlefield, while in Virginia the trail traces the Blue Ridge where I trekked when I was in college in Charlottesville just a few miles away.

The Appalachian Trail is both wild in its route and, at the same time, accessible to East Coasters, often just an hour or so drive away from major cities. The trail was founded in the 1920s, with the first stretch in New York State running from Bear Mountain down into New Jersey. It is marked with white splashes of paint on rocks or trees every fifty feet or so, and it is well-trodden—less a path in a forest and more a carved out way where two hikers can easily pass by. There are three types of hikers on the trail. There is the through-hiker whose goal is to hike the full extent. There is the segment hiker, who might be on a three day or week-long hike, perhaps choosing to hike the trail within or across a single state. And then there are the hikers like myself, who are out for a day to get away from things.

I decided to hike the Appalachian trail early this summer, but life got in the way a bit. My ambition was to do a four-day segment hike in New Jersey and New York, but as the summer season zoomed by with seeming higher priorities, my plan devolved into just sampling the trail on a day hike. On a September Thursday, I drove out to western New Jersey and parked at the Delaware Water Gap National Recreation Area parking lot, where the Appalachian Trail crosses from Pennsylvania into northern New Jersey. I filled my backpack with lunch, a water bottle, and a detailed trail map. I was tight on time and worried about my conditioning, so I thought two hours out and two hours back would be the right amount.

The hike went off, but not without some hitches. Because I began at river level, most of the hike out was uphill while the way back sloped back down. The trail itself, at 90 years old, was worn down. The path had almost no topsoil to make it smooth but consisted almost entirely of rocks, which meant that at times I had to wind my way around the stones or, in other instances hop from one stone to another. This was not a problem heading uphill where the rocks provided purchase, nor downhill where I could hop and glide down from rock to rock. The stones were the biggest problem on more level parts of the path, where they broke up the cadence of my steps.

About two miles into the walk, I spotted a black bear 400 feet ahead on the path. It was not too large, perhaps 150 or 200 pounds, but the sight of the bear stopped me in my tracks. It had not noticed me and seemed to be rooting around for something. Not wanting to give up on my hike and not wanting to go around the bear (it was a rugged section of the trail), I began waving my hands and yelling. The bear looked up and spotted me. We shared a brief stare-down; in retrospect probably both of us were terrified. Happily though for both of us, the bear soon turned and sprinted off the path up a nearby hill and out of sight. Belying its size, the bear moved with incredible speed and reminded me of a jackrabbit. What scared me less was the bear's presence on the path, and more the fact that the bear could move much faster than I ever could. I was not really in control of the situation.

And I think that may be the point of a mountain hike. When we walk on a neighborhood sidewalk or in our local parks, we are in a landscape orchestrated for our use. The land is pre-designed. Our path has been chosen; the routes demarcated and sized for human scale and sensibility. When we head out on actual hiking trails, we encounter a more unmediated nature, a natural world indifferent to our intent and sensibility. The rocks that I trod upon are half a billion years old and are indifferent to my suffering. I am a momentary blip in the eons of nature. The path dictates our destiny. We climb a trail upwards that momentarily exhausts us and causes us to pause, and we then descend just as steeply, providing a thrill of danger as we head down. The bear chose to run away, but could quickly have veered towards me with speed. It is not us against nature, but nature confronting us with the fact of its existence while we, with our small intentions, perform our little play.

After venturing up Mount Katahdin in Maine, Henry David Thoreau wrote, "I first most fully realized that this was unhanselled (sic) and ancient Demonic Nature, natura, or whatever man has named it...nature primitive—powerful, gigantic, aweful and beautiful." This encounter with such a big, untamed, unperturbed natural world is the point of a hike. We are humbled in our efforts to conquer this world, and this humility in the face of nature can reset our psyches and give us an appreciation for our place in larger space and time. At the end of the hike we are relieved of the pressure of this confrontation with nature, but the encounter has left us better off. We have accomplished a feat. We are enervated by the effort, but are uplifted in spirit as we are more in touch with the essential.

ESSAI 12
Vocabulary

I like to walk about amidst the beautiful things that adorn the world.

—*George Santayana*

It is no wonder that we have so many words for walking. It is the physical activity that makes us humans most human. We step, stride, march, run, and gallop. We can go forth, proceed, advance, and make headway. We amble, ramble, and wander. We tramp and traverse. We can promenade, I guess if we are out on a promenade. If this was 1800s England, we could 'take a turn' escorting a paramour around the garden. We can meander like a small stream. We can perambulate in circles. We can, as the B-52s sang, "roam if you want to; roam around the world."

The word 'walk' itself is ubiquitous and diverse. If I was in the military, I could walk the wall or walk the boundary. A cop walks the beat. Down under, I could go on a walkabout in the Outback. Pirates would make me walk the plank, or if I had too much grog, perhaps they would let me walk it off. Some have asked me my walk of life, and someday I may have to explain why I was given my walking papers.

Sometimes we walk with more determination. Soldiers and protesters march, which suggests multiple walkers, moving in sync with purpose and a common rhythm. There are marching songs designed to ensure the cadence of the group, and likely to relieve boredom. Marchers often have lost their freedom, as a troublemaker can get "marched out the door." We name the month of March for Mars, the god of war. Borderlands in England were once labeled "marches" reflecting need for soldiers to patrol borders.

Often our walks become more rigorous, in which case we designate them, sometimes too proudly, as hikes. Walkers wear shoes or sneakers, but hikers must wear boots to deal with more rugged ground. "Hike" derives from the older English word "hyke" which means to walk vigorously. In old Scottish, "hyke" meant to move with a jerk, and the Germanic derivation suggests walking with a limp or hopping. We do not walk smoothly on a hike, but climb up or down in elevation, or over or around obstacles. The idea of our bodies getting jerked around in hiking makes good sense. When the center hikes the football to the quarterback, he jerks it quickly backward,

We ratchet down our determination when we decide to just roam or wander. In wandering, we give up a fixed course and go hither and tither. We stray from the set path. When we wander, we summon our wherewithal to wind or wend our way willfully unwilling. There is a curvature to our wandering or roaming. The closest distance between two points is a straight line, but we have decided that the endpoint is not the goal when we roam. The journey itself deserves more time and more randomness. When my mind wanders, it daydreams and departs from the rational, and on our wandering paths, we similarly open ourselves up to differentness and newness. A section of Central Park in New York City, the Ramble, was designed for this type of walking where we are not quite sure where we are headed. The Ramble consists of meandering, crisscrossing paths deep in a wooded area. There are streams and hills, and we lose our sense of direction. We get discombobulated and give ourselves up to just walking with uncertainty.

All types of walking require steps and strides. Steps are the most tightly-defined and smallest increments of walking. It is the way we measure—if that is our intent—the length of the walks that we take. "Step" is a short, onomatopoeic word that matches its meaning as a singular placement of one leg and foot forward. The sibilant start of the term "step," the "st," matches the quiet lifting of the foot at the beginning of a step, while the harder "p" at the end reflects the staccato landing of our shoe ahead onto the ground.

Step counters work by registering that slight jerk at the end of every step. Many of us use step counters to measure and feel a sense of accomplishment for walking during the day. We appreciate step counters because of the sheer number of our steps we take, one hundred million throughout a lifetime. The step counters, especially the ones connected to health apps, are, in a way, designed to remind us that steps are essential, more stepping out (and less sitting down) is what we are anatomically designed to do. Time moves forward in one-second increments, as we move forward with our steps each day.

Striding is stepping on steroids. It is a longer stretch of the leg, suggesting more urgency of intent and perhaps more pomposity than simple steps. Strides announce themselves to the world. A striding person on the sidewalk can be disruptive because they are moving at a different speed than the rest of us. Striding is strident, in that it can be harsh and grating to others around us. Egotistically, though, when we hit our stride, we are often at the high point of our performance: shit is getting done!

What happens when a walk goes bad? Well, it becomes a slog which requires us to toil as we trod or tromp, or to traipse while we schlep, or just plod. As we mosey along, it is best not to delay by dawdling, but rather to glide or perhaps sashay as we stretch our legs. A march is often dispositive, as in "Sherman's March to the Sea" through Georgia, or the World War II "Bataan Death March" in the Philippines. Our walks can indeed be horrendous. When outside forces intervene, it takes extra strength to continue forward and not lose momentum.

The word, "walk," comes from the Old English word "wealcan" which means tossing, rolling, or moving around. The history of the word "walk," and its use in different forms and spelling in other languages, include the sense of the turning, the kneading or the rolling of cloth or dough. A walk can be transformative, less about striding, eyes rigidly forward, but more about turning from side to side in wonder. As I walk forward, I am figuratively kneading my psyche, softening it so that it is quieter and more in the present moment and making it ready to rise in the heat of the activities later in the day.

My favorite word for a walk is the "constitutional," as in, "Time for me to take my daily constitutional!" The constitutional is seen as something that is good for one's constitution, one's physical and mental health. It presupposes that we all have constitutions, or perhaps a core thing about us that needs sustenance or needs some tuning up. To misquote our founding document: "We the people in order to be more perfect, establish tranquility, and express our liberty, need to ordain and establish a daily constitutional." So let's go forth--head high, striding or ambling, counting our steps, on a hike or even promenade!

ESSAI 13
Quads (and more UVa)

On prospect I have a rich profusion...at every point of the compass. Mountains distant and near, smooth and shaggy, single and in ridges, a little river hiding itself among hills...cultivated grounds under the eye and two small villages.

—Thomas Jefferson

When I was a student in college, I walked much more than I do now. I walked everywhere, from my apartment to class, from one academic building to the next, from classrooms to the student union, from the student union to the library, and on and on. Many colleges, including the University of Virginia, where I was an undergraduate, have campuses. A university is not a single building but many, spread out like a village or small town with streets or walkways between them, and open grassy areas like public parks sweeping from one structure to the next. Students and professors can cross a campus end to end in 15 minutes or so. A typical campus is about a square mile in size. As colleges have grown into universities, they sometimes have multiple campuses ('campi'?) with buses to cross the greater distances. The word campus comes to us from Ancient Rome and connotes a field where games are played, public festivities occur, and militias mustered. The "Campus Martius" in

Rome was an open area just outside the city comprising several square kilometers and serving as a catch-all venue for horse races, religious festivities, and civic gatherings. Back then, a "campus" was both very public and very open. Princeton University began using the word to describe their grounds in 1774, purposefully contrasting their rural setting to the more urban, cloistered schools in Europe.

The big quads are where the action takes place at our most historic universities. Harvard has its "Yard," a stately lawn with majestic trees, surrounded mostly by student housing. At Dartmouth, it is the "Green," which sweeps up from the town to Dartmouth Hall up on the hill. At some schools like Boston College or Tulane, it is known simply as "the quad." At the University of Virginia, there is Jefferson's historic "Lawn," bordered by student and professor housing and connecting classic colonnades.

Jefferson's quad, his Lawn, was the centerpiece of his vision for a new type of university, one which was different from what came before and what has since followed.* Part of Jefferson's design for the University of Virginia reflected problems that he saw in his alma mater, William and Mary College. His vision for the university was to create a more well-rounded educational experience—an enhanced environment in a better part of the state than what William and Mary offered. Jefferson once referred to the architecture of William and Mary as "rude, misshapen piles, which, but they have roofs, would be taken for brick kilns." This aesthetic dislike was compounded by his aversion to the college's location in the humid tidewater region. Since he had attended William and Mary forty years prior, the population of Virginia had grown and shifted more to the interior part of the state, closer to Charlottesville, where Jefferson's home, Monticello, was located. Williamsburg was no longer the state capital and was in decline. The opportunity was ripe for creating a new university, and Jefferson who was finishing his second presidential term envisioned creating a university near his home in Charlottesville as a capstone project for his life of service.

Jefferson had a unique vision of the process of education, rooted in the idea of mentorship and the proper relation between professor and student. In his own studies, Jefferson had benefitted from the mentorship of teachers and politicians in the 1760s, developing close personal relationships with the likes of Francis Fauquier and William Small. Jefferson paid this back in later years as he mentored a younger generation of politicians, explorers, and scientists. James Madison, Merriweather Lewis, William Short, James Monroe, and Jefferson's own sons and grandsons are just a few examples.** Jefferson also had the examples of Plato's academy and the Stoics, for the desired the closeness and informality of the philosopher/follower relationship enhanced by living together and sharing a common garden, separated from the hubbub of the town or city.

For his university plan, Jefferson sought to enhance the connection between student and professor via the architectural design itself. He wanted closeness among students and teachers but wanted to avoid a single, large structure where everyone would live. Jefferson admired the layout and social fabric of New England villages, which he toured with James Madison in the 1890s. He felt that the idea of a community with its cluster of dwellings, a common meeting place, and town meetings created mini-democracies. Practically, Jefferson wished to avoid having just a single large building to mitigate the spread of disease and the risk of fire.

For the University of Virginia, Jefferson embraced the idea of an "Academical Village" as the key design concept that would facilitate liberty and freedom of thought while maintaining just enough of the professor/student hierarchical relationship. In Jefferson's concept, student rooms would be attached to professors' houses (the pavilions) by covered walkways to facilitate a domestic, tutorial style of education. Classically, pupils would cluster around their professor—they would learn from him, dine with him, and, in a way, be like sons to him.

Taking the concept further, the student rooms and professor houses would surround a grassy lawn bordered by native trees, reminiscent of a quiet country landscape that could facilitate contemplation and study. In pleasant weather, the students could meet in the central grassy area, perhaps study the surrounding architectural styles, and acquire knowledge in quiet communion with nature.

Location and siting mattered as well. As with Jefferson's other architectural designs, the university bears the definitive stamp of Italian architect Andrea Palladio. Palladio's "Four Books of Architecture" can almost be used as a guidebook when studying Jefferson's architecture. Palladio suggests locating structures, "where the mind, fatigued by the agitations of the city will be greatly restored and comforted, and be able to quietly attend the studies of letters and contemplations." Jefferson located the University in rural Albermarle county, away from Richmond or Washington D.C., to create that contemplative separation. Palladio also emphasized architectural siting as critical, suggesting that one should "build upon elevated and chearful (sic) places, where the air is, by the continual blowing of winds, moved." Palladio further warns not to build in valleys, but at higher elevations, to allow "seeing at a distance, and of being seen." Jefferson took this advice to heart, first with his home Monticello (the name itself meaning "little mountain") and then with the university. The Rotunda at the university crowns a hill and can be seen from all sides, and from the steps of the Rotunda or from the windows on the top level, one in turn can see out to a full view of the Virginia countryside. This idea of the grandeur of viewing served an educational intention to elevate students' sensibilities and inspire the educational experience.

This concern with view and sight can best be seen in the visual trick incorporated into the design of the Academical Village. Standing at the Rotunda's front entrance and looking down the length of the Lawn, it appears as if all the pavilion buildings are evenly spaced. In actuality, Jefferson left successively larger spaces between the pavilions as they extended down the Lawn. This creates the illusion when looking from the Rotunda that the buildings are evenly sited (and is reminiscent of the architectural tricks then prevalent in 17th-century French classical gardens). Jefferson was preoccupied with looking outwards from the hilltop Rotunda onto the rolling piedmont landscape. The view captures his village design in the pastoral setting of his home county. Jefferson kept the plan simple: the Lawn is a simple open rectangle.

A walk through Jefferson's Academical Village is a bit bizarre. One can only approach the Lawn by coming uphill from behind the architecture or from below the Rotunda. Once upon the Lawn itself, it feels most appropriate to keep off the grass and walk along the colonnades connecting the pavilions—the site exudes a sense of history and even holiness. But, in walking along the colonnades, one misses the bulk of the classic architecture, and the lawn's aesthetic experience is essentially hidden. Only when one ventures a bit bravely out onto the lawn itself can one see the pavilion and Rotunda architecture and take in the grandeur of the entire village. And I think this was Jefferson's intent. To experience the full aesthetic requires a climb from the mundane back alleys of the site, through the architecture, and only then out onto the greensward. Intent is required and effort is rewarded, and we feel a bit transformed by the experience and prepared to learn more.

It is critical to emphasize again how problematic it is that Jefferson's educational vision did not include African Americans or women, and that slave labor was used to construct a university intended initially only for sons of the white planter and professional class.

**With his mixed race Hemings sons, Jefferson sought to ensure that each had a trade to rely on. This fact remains non-exculpatory.*

ESSAI 14
Sherman's March

Courage — a perfect sensibility of the measure of
danger, and a mental willingness to endure it.
—William Tecumseh Sherman

There is something about the intensity of the Civil War — the stakes for both sides, the scale of the geography, the great personalities, and the intricacies of strategy. Recently I've been engrossed by Civil War generals, making my way through the classic autobiography of Ulysses S. Grant, where Grant gives us both the quotidian and drama of war while revealing his sensibility.

Following Grant, I turned to the memoir of that other great Union general, William Tecumseh Sherman.* Sherman's generalship during the Civil War was infamous. "War is cruelty," Sherman wrote in his memoirs, and his army's devastating 250-mile trek across the Georgia countryside from Atlanta eastwards to Savannah -- the "March to the Sea" --was the penultimate act in the war. Sherman's march sapped the will of the Confederacy and presaged the final surrender by Lee four months later.

This is all big historical stuff, but what caught my eye in Sherman's memoirs was his recounting of a seemingly innocuous trip he took 30 years before the Civil War. In 1836, the 17-year-old Sherman traveled 700 miles from his home in Lancaster, Ohio to go to college at the U.S. Military Academy at West Point on the Hudson River 50 miles north of New York City. Sherman described the places he stayed in and the people he saw in some detail, and he provided an accounting of all of his modes of transportation too. The trip took about a month, including some longer stops in Washington, D.C. Sherman wrote more about those four days of travel than he did about his entire four following years at West Point. His descriptions are highly specific, calling out details like the street locations of homes he visited during the trip (C Street, Arch Street, White Street) and the names of hotels where he stayed (Gadsby, American, Mansion House). This is remarkable given Sherman published the memoir 50 years after the fact.

Sherman built his story as if tracing his journey on a map, marking his route across the geography as he traveled by boat, by rail, and by coach. At that time, the country was in the midst of a transportation revolution, and Sherman captures the sense of a modernizing United States. Sherman's journey from the west (Ohio) to the east (Washington) and then north to New York was the inverse of the westward thrust of Manifest Destiny. This was a young man from the west heading east, and, in this reverse route, we can see Sherman moving from his more rural, small-town home to an industrializing, north-eastern world. Sherman's description of the trip gives it the aura of a quest. The journey for Sherman had an epic flavor with twists, turns, and chance encounters. Indeed, the trip depicts Sherman's curiosity and determination, presaging the military campaigns he would conduct three decades later.

Planning for the journey began in 1836 when Sherman received his formal appointment to the U.S. Military Academy from the Secretary of War. Stage one of his trip would be from Ohio to Washington, D.C., where he would visit his guardian,

Thomas Ewing, a U.S. Senator from Ohio at that time (Sherman's father had died seven years earlier). Sherman first made his way from his Lancaster home to Zanesville, Ohio, just 45 miles to the east. At that time, Zanesville was a stage-coach stop on the famous and historic "National Road." Twenty years before, Albert Gallatin, the Secretary of the Treasury under both Presidents Jefferson and Madison conceived the National Road as the first federally funded and built road, the first national highway in the United States. Gallatin hoped to provide an east-west road, crossing the Appalachians to connect the coastal states to the Ohio Country, supplanting what were primarily just forest trails as the only routes. Construction had begun in 1811, and, by the 1830s, the road extended into Ohio. Sherman spent just three days on the road, riding fast stagecoaches over its smoothed, macadam** surface from eastern Ohio across northwestern Virginia and into Maryland. Stopping at Frederick, Maryland, midway through the state, Sherman faced a choice: he could take the newfangled railroad to Baltimore and thence to Washington, or he could go by horse carriage faster straight across country. Reminiscent of his later campaigning in Georgia, Sherman opted for speed and surety, choosing the speedy and direct coach route. "Not having full faith in the novel and dangerous railroad, I stuck to the coach," wrote Sherman.

Sherman stayed a week in Washington, where we can see the forthrightness and curiosity of his later fame. Sherman took advantage of his status as the ward of Thomas Ewing, a prominent senator at that time. He made it a point to see some of the great politicians of the era, including Henry Clay, John Calhoun, Daniel Webster, President Andrew Jackson, and Vice President (later President) Martin Van Buren. Then, Sherman was off to New York via Philadelphia.

Leaving Washington for New York, Sherman finally did opt

for the "novel and dangerous" train, taking the B&O railroad up to Baltimore and then a boat across the Susquehanna River to Havre de Grace, Maryland. The train continued to Wilmington and the Delaware Bay, where Sherman again disembarked for a boat up the Delaware River to Philadelphia. The early railroads were discontinuous along the East Coast because of the many river crossings and lack of bridges at that time. On his trip from Washington to his eventual endpoint in New York, Sherman would boat or ferry across four significant rivers. It would be another 30 years, for example, before the Susquehanna was finally bridged.

After a brief stay in Philadelphia, Sherman took yet another boat up the Delaware River to Bordentown, New Jersey, just south of Trenton. There, Sherman boarded the C&A (Camden and Amboy) railroad up to Amboy, New Jersey, below Staten Island. The C&A railroad was just 5 years old and was the first steam railroad in North America. The C&A route allowed goods and people to travel from one water terminus (Bordentown, close to the falls of the Delaware River on the west side of New Jersey) to another (Amboy, on the east side of New Jersey, where the Raritan River emptied into the Raritan and New York Bays). From Amboy, Sherman could take a last boat ride the short distance up to New York Harbor. After staying a week in New York, visiting with two of his uncles, Sherman took the final leg of his journey 50 miles up the Hudson to West Point. He traveled cheaply on a steamship owned by Cornelius Vanderbilt, who was building his transportation empire at that time.

Here is an intrepid youth, who routed himself through three great cities and connected with family, friends, and some famed politicians along the way. We see Sherman's practical willingness to experiment on his journey with different modes of transportation. We also see detail and clarity in his descriptions. This was not just a trip to school, but a foreshadowing of the famed general to come. Sherman trekked from west to east—both in this first journey of his life and in his vast army's Georgia march 30 years hence, with purpose, practicality, curiosity, and adventure.

*"Great" from a northern point of view, less so for the South.

**The "macadam" road type was the early 19th century brainchild of the Scottish engineer John Loudon McAdam, who devised a raised road surface, slightly arched and covered with a compacted layer of smaller stones that would allow for runoff. The smaller stones would compact further over time with use. Macadam roads solved for issues with the mud and ruts of dirt roads, and the bumpiness of larger cobbled stones.

ESSAI 15
Disconnection and Reconnection

In every walk with nature one receives far more than he seeks.

—*John Muir*

We are disconnected from nature. We see the natural world as something separate from us, a stage for human activity, a tool to be used, a source of energy for our purposes. It often feels like we are in conflict with nature, viciously fracking oil from the ground, blanketing the oceans with islands of plastic, and amping up the weather with our carbon emissions.

Humans exert their dominance over the earth's resources on a large scale, but also in quotidian ways. We manicure our domestic and business landscapes, over-watering and over-fertilizing lawns and garden beds. We deploy weed and insect-killing chemicals not just in our agriculture but on our sidewalks where we walk the dog and where our children play. We work to prohibit the intrusion of the natural world in our lives, creating a wedge between us and the untempered environment. In doing so, we create pain for our environment and (I would argue) for ourselves too. We experience a deep nostalgia for past times and for experiences that re-embed us in nature. In this essai, I hope to explore the genesis of this separation between us and nature and perhaps generate some thinking about reconnecting and reestablishing a more holistic conception of ourselves and the world around us.

Many pre-historic cultures conceived of nature and god as one. Humans saw nature and divinity as coincident: god was nature and nature was god, and the human place in this god/nature world was inherent and indivisible. In this conception, humans were part of a holistic nature-divinity continuum. This perspective is quite different than our modern belief in the anthropomorphic, distinct-from-nature gods in many of today's religions. We have moved away from the holistic idea of nature/god/man of pre-civilization, and into a world of division.

We feel stress from the absence of nature in our lives, and we long for it, as evidenced by how we see it portrayed as an ideal in many films and books. The 2009 film, "Avatar," depicts a sci-fi fantasy world where all animals and plants (excluding the human invaders) play out their existence in concert with each other, with an intrinsic connection of their souls to the plants and the land itself. In the film, flora and fauna and the environment are one and imbued with a sacred spirit. The human corporation that has visited the planet, along with its military and scientific adjuncts, finds this connectedness incomprehensible. They look to extract natural resources from the planet through strip mining. We see two different ways of life: one that is joyful, soulful, and in sync with nature, and another that is harsh and in conflict with it. We see this in our world when we compare modern and premodern cultures. Something in history happened to our sensibilities about nature, where we moved from a divine belief of life to seeing nature transactionally.

Before the advent of farming, nature was simply wilderness. Hunter-gatherers would not have seen the distinction between wilderness and civilization, between uncultivated and cultivated. We were wild, and we lived in the wild hunting and consuming animals, and gathering seeds, fruits, leaves, and roots for sustenance. This primeval nature was undeveloped, immersive, and unmediated. Ancient human cultures often conceived of the natural world as maternal and worshipped different manifestations of the "earth goddess." Earth goddess worship was quite different from our religions today. The earth goddess symbolized the fruitfulness of the earth: the analogy of seeds planted in the ground leading to nascence and growth. Earth was the mother that gives birth to plants, animals, and people. This goddess was not a separate thing from the world or nature; all life was seen as the actual manifestation of the goddess.

Although earth-goddess worship held less sway after the advent of agriculture and the emergence of early civilizations, traces of the idea remained in familiar mythologies. The Greek goddess Hera represented the earth and its fruitfulness, and indeed the other Greek goddesses manifested different facets of nature as well. Even today, we still think of "Mother Nature," and deep down, we perhaps desire that intimate parent-child relationship with the earth.

So what happened to our original, holistic, mother-earth conception of nature? What caused this idea of the divinity of the world to no longer hold sway? The emergence of civilization built around plant agriculture and husbandry necessitated a change in the view of nature, from immersion and co-identity to separateness and control. With agriculture, especially large-scale farming which required organized irrigation efforts, humans moved to exert control over their environment and adopt the role of steward or master of the land.

We see the genesis of this thinking in the Judeo-Christian "Garden of Eden" story. The Garden is a paradise, but it is not unmediated nature. It is not wild. Eden is a pastoral land designed for humans and intended for them to live an ideal life. Paradise was not the old wilderness, but a pre-designed plot of land. In the Eden story, the Garden is not seen as divine, but rather as a separate entity that God designed and implemented.

With the conception of Eden, we see that god, nature, and humans are no longer connected, but act and behave separately with diverse intent. Our role is now to use the land to his purpose, and in fact, God commands just that. In Genesis 1:28: "God said unto them, Be fruitful, and multiply, and replenish the earth, and subdue it: and have dominion over the fish of the sea, and over the fowl of the air, and over every living thing that moveth upon the earth." God similarly told Adam to till the land. God and Man are artisanal. God creates the world in six days, and then Adam and Eve are placed in a stewardship over it. In this sense, humans are no longer of nature. Early ideas of harmony and co-existence have been replaced with pejorative words like "subdue" and "dominion," allowing exploitation of the environment.

The eventual betrayal of even this nature that occurs with the biting of the apple further heightens the separation between humans and nature. Paradise (Eden) is now lost and becomes instead something to regain, an ideal to strive for. Adam and Eve are cast out into the wilderness, and they and their descendants have to fight with nature and control it to their use, seeking to recreate the Eden that they lost.

With the emergence of early civilizations, humans looked to reorder the natural world, seeking to Eden-ize the wilderness for their use. With the advent of agriculture, we cleared the ancient forests, plotted out geometric farming areas, sowed straight furrows, built fences for livestock, erected villages and walls, and began linking communities through roads. The land was tamed, controlled for our use, intended to be made a "paradise," not of wilderness untamed, but of territory controlled for our utility and delight.

This seeking to recreate Eden is not the desire for the raw wilderness ideal; it is the nature of the agricultural countryside, of farms and animal-husbandry. It is the rolling landscape of farmhouses and barns set amidst fields green with crops. It is wooden corrals for horses, or pastures dotted with sheep or cows quietly grazing. The aesthetic of farmland feels genuinely natural. Although it is filled with plants and animals, pastoral land is still created by humans for humans. It is nature refined for human sensibility. The earth is no longer intrinsically divine, yet there is an ideal of a pastoral "Eden" that still exists and that we yearn for.

We, therefore, live with two conceptions of nature. There is the nature of the wilderness—of the primeval, untamed forests, mountains, and rivers, and there is also the more recent pastoral nature of the countryside, farms, and pastures. Both of these conceptions are premodern, and are now violated by the introduction of modern industrial technologies.

We still long for the wilderness. It is no wonder that Theodore Roosevelt, our greatest wilderness conservation president, grew up in urban New York. As President, Roosevelt set aside 230,000,000 acres, mostly western lands, to remain preserved, creating five new national parks. For the last hundred years, there has been a value placed on setting aside remaining wilderness lands not only as plant and animal sanctuaries, but also for people to venture into. Hiking, camping, and mountain-climbing in untouched areas have become an end in itself as a way to escape from our highly designed cities and sophisticated technologies to instill self-abnegation and regain a sense of humility and awe.

The desire for wilderness is quite different from what we seek when we visit rustic farm country. Here it is less about the awesome power of nature and more about a feeling of nostalgia for a simpler, bucolic past. For many of us, this means venturing out to the countryside to drive by farms, look at fall colors, pick fruit from orchards, and stop at roadside vegetable stands. We are not interested in viewing farming per se, especially the vast factory farms of the Midwest and Plains states. We are more interested in re-immersing ourselves in a countryside settled by farmers in the late 18th and early 19th century with red barns, stone walls, and clapboard farmhouses. We want to drive or bike or walk through this type of land, and then visit a local village and perhaps shop for antiques or books. We seek vicarious access to an idealized past that taps a subliminal chord.

Within cities and suburbs we further hearken to the past by shaping and architecting the land in an idealistic way. We try to bring islands of Eden into our urban worlds through architecture and landscape planning. Whether it is houses surrounded by their lawns and gardens, apartment buildings with grassy courtyards, office parks designed like college campuses, or town commons and village squares, we work to strike a balance between development for shelter, work, or play while still retaining the feel of the natural world. We feel a need to have grassy greenswards bordered by majestic trees with paths that meander around. New York's Central Park, with its vast lawns, century-old trees, and winding lanes, is the ultimate expression of placing the pastoral in the urban, and, in the last half century, there are further examples. Old mills, piers, and canals are now repurposed as nature parks with grasses, shrubs, and wildflowers seemingly running rampant, but they are actually carefully orchestrated daily by gardeners. The elevated High Line railway in New York City, once just an industrial blight that wove its way through factories and warehouses, is now a walking garden as nature is embedded into the architecture.

We clearly want to have our cake and eat it too. We love our machines, our buildings, our industry, and our technology. The steel and glass behemoth of the Seagram's building on Park Avenue in New York, the container ship loading/unloading complex in Elizabeth, New Jersey, or the smartphone in our left pocket feel far from primeval or pastoral nature. But we also deeply desire the contrasting feel of nature. Whereas in the past, we had islands of urban development in the broad farming countryside or even amidst wilderness, today it feels more like we have small islands of nature dotting an entirely manufactured landscape. These small islands are treasured because, deep down, these natural landscapes feel more true to us, physically and psychologically. The way the modern world overwhelms us demands that we look again to nature and rediscover our own lives in the process. Whether it is the nostalgia of walking through a park or more in-depth immersion in the wilderness, we can reconnect to a broader sense of wonder or even the divinity that humans once believed in.

ESSAI 16
Measurement

The journey of a thousand miles begins with a single step.

—Lao Tze

There has always been resistance to the metric system in the United States. Despite decades of effort by thousands of teachers, the traditional, old-world measurements of distance and area still stick around. I think this is because the old measurements and even the names themselves are more intuitive to our experience of landscape. Metric system naming is too logical sounding and too sterile, with words like liter and meter modified by suffixes like kilo and mili. There is a French or perhaps Latinate feel to the metric vocabulary, which feels foreign in the way the words reverberate in our minds, almost with a metallic clang.

The old words are better. Walking a "kilometer" fails to resonate, while the fifteen-minute jaunt of a "mile" invigorates. There is a human scale to the old measurements. Less than a mile is not really a walk (more a stroll), while distances longer than a mile require extra resolution and preparation. Even the word "mile" connotes about a thousand or so strides. "How far?" "Not far, just a mile."

When we have many miles to travel, we could use the

old term, "league." A league represents different distances in different countries, ranging from two-and-a-half to four-and-a-half miles. The rule of thumb in Great Britain now is that a league is three miles. It feels old school to talk about leagues. Christopher Columbus described his first view of the island of San Salvador as "...extending from north to south five leagues, and the other side which we coasted along, ran from east to west more than ten leagues." Jules Verne's 1870 novel had Captain Nemo traveling 20,000 leagues under the sea, which is 60,000 miles, or roughly two-and-a-half times around the earth. We can walk one league in about an hour, or run a league, which is the almost exact equivalent of all of those sterile sounding 5K races which plague our community calendars, in 20 or 30 minutes. I think I would rather hike a league across the countryside than run a 5K on a high school track.

Smaller distances are more in our grasp. Watching the Kentucky Derby this year, I heard an announcer talk about "furlongs." I looked it up. A mile has eight furlongs, and a league would have twenty-four. A furlong stretches 220 yards, and the name comes from the combination of two words: "furrow" and "long." A furlong is the same length as a traditional row of tilled land, at least back before tractors and combines. Furlong is mostly obsolete but crops up, as mentioned, in thoroughbred racing. The Kentucky Derby at 1-1/4 miles is an even 10 furlongs distance, while the other two legs of the Triple Crown are 9.5 furlongs (The Preakness) and 12 furlongs (The Belmont Stakes). It is no wonder each year that some horses win the two shorter distance races but fail at the longer Belmont given the horse has to run two more farm field lengths.

An "acre" as it turns out, was originally a furlong in length and about four "poles" (twenty-two yards) wide. Each "pole" or "rod" is five-and-a-half yards long and may have been based on the old length of an ox goad. The name "acre" comes from the Latin "ager" or Old English "aecer" -- both of which meant "field." An acre was a field based on the area that a team of oxen could plow in a single day. The original furlong-long, four-pole-wide rectangle shape of the acre was 10 times longer than wide. It made plowing easier as the oxen had to turn around less often during the day.

The area of an acre is 43,560 square feet and is 1/640th of a square mile. By the early 1800s, the acre in the United States morphed from the old strip-like, oblong shape to one that was more like a square. There were two reasons for this. First, fencing in land became critical to restrict cattle from roaming into crop fields or to keep the cattle themselves penned. Given the effort required to fence fields, farmers chose square areas to save the time and cost of longer fences. A square acre requires just 835 feet of fence, while the original furlong length acre would require 1,452 feet of fence. A second driver of square fields and square acres, was the U.S. Land Ordinance of 1785, which was the federal law that mandated the square grid system for the old Northwest Territory (today's Midwestern states). Square townships, dictated by the Land Ordinance, begat square farm plots based on square acres. U.S. law defined a township as 36 square miles, each square mile of which comprises 640 acres. A new township thus had 23,040 acres of land or enough for 400 or so 40-acre farms. Back then, green acres were the place to be.

The "acre," of course, remains a handy way to call out property size, not just for farms, but for suburbs. Towns often create uniform neighborhood lots based on acres or portions of acres, which makes tax assessment easier. Potential homeowners place value on lot size defined by acreage. Surveyors measure our plots of land in both the U.S. and Canada using a Surveyor's Chain, also known as "Gunter's Chain." The Gunter's Chain was invented in the 1600s by the English mathematician Edmund Gunter. It is 22 yards long and has 100 links. An area of 10 square chains equals one square acre, so a chain provides both a manageable way to physically measure land segments and show finer divisions of an acre in smaller lots or in lots not truly square.

Something is pleasing about the size of an acre today. A house on an acre includes enough land to surround the house and provides enough area for activity—the kids can run in the sprinkler! Many of our sports take up about an acre. Twenty four men can roughhouse on the acre of football gridiron (where if they advance the ball ten yards, they "move the chains.") Twenty-two women can get a kick from playing on an acre of a soccer pitch. Eighteen Little Leaguers can pitch and hit on their acre too. We can garden on our acre, walk a mile to the store, or trek two leagues across our township—the measure of land in the measure of us.

Linear Measures:
12 inches = 1 foot
3 feet = 1 yard
5.5 yard = 1 rod or pole (16.5 feet)
40 rods = 1 furlong (220 yards)
8 furlongs = 1 mile
3 miles = 1 league

Surveying Measures Linear:
7.92 inches = 1 link
100 links = 1 chain (Gunter's Chain, 66 feet)
80 chains = 1 mile (5280 feet)

Surveying Measures Area:
625 square links = 1 square pole or square rod
10 square rods = 1 square chain
10 square chains = 1 acre
640 acres = 1 square mile
36 square miles = 1 township

ESSAI 17
Tolkien's Landscape

I wisely started with a map and made the story fit.
—*J.R.R. Tolkien*

When asked what my favorite book is, I answer without hesitation that it is *The Lord of the Rings*. My love for J.R.R. Tolkien's epic immediately characterizes me as a member of the nerdy, escapist class of readers that hearkens to fantasy and science-fiction novels. This is true, and I don't care.

For years, from age 10 well into my mid-20s, I would often read for hours a day, pushing away the world and indulging my introversion. I remember reading *The Lord of the Rings* (LOTR) for the first time all the way through in 1977, sitting in one of the two orange chairs in our family living room in Huntington, Long Island, drinking Lipton Iced tea, and shutting out the understandable mayhem of a house with five brothers and sisters. Since then, I have reread the book,* and its prequels, *The Hobbit* and *The Simarillion* at least a dozen times. I even took a course in college on Tolkien and his fellow fantasy writer C.S. Lewis.

What is it that makes me come back over and over to Tolkien's world? I think, at first, I relished the high-action plot: the journey through danger, the sword fights, and the large battle scenes. Later I began to appreciate the depth of Tolkien's literary craft, the care he took in creating a highly-detailed, complete history of his fantasy world of Middle-earth, with stories and timelines stretching from that world's creation to the present day of the novel. Along with the history, Tolkien showed a deep love of words and languages, derived from his studies of Norse and Old English as a philologist and professor of medieval literature. There was a deep satisfaction with the story itself, which captured the hero's journey of both Frodo the Hobbit and of Aragorn, the would-be king, including their willingness to sacrifice and their devotion to friendship.

It's not just me. Tolkien published *The Lord of the Rings* in 1954 and 1955, and it holds place as perhaps the best-loved piece of English literature from the 20th century. Sales of the book have topped 150 million, and it has been translated into 50 languages. The film adaptations over the last decade and a half have produced over $5 billion in revenue, and the third installment of the series received the Academy Award for Best Picture.

Tolkien gave us the epic tale of Frodo Baggins and his hobbit companions (Sam, Pippin, and Merry) and their quest to destroy the great Ring of Power and keep it from the clutches of the Dark Lord Sauron. A parallel story is the rise of the Ranger Aragorn and his return to his rightful place as king of western men. Tolkien shows a journey of growth for each of his principal characters as they travel from their homes through forests, over rivers and valleys, and through mountains and caves, while meeting friends and fighting or escaping from foes.

Although the story and the characters draw most of the attention in the books and in the films, Tolkien spent as much time devising the geography of Middle-earth, creating an intentional landscape that resonated with historical, medieval, and biblical themes. Tolkien devoted incredible attention to establishing his world, providing detailed maps for the reader.

While his son, Christopher Tolkien, drew the final charts for the publication, Tolkien took on the role of artist, providing the cover art for all three volumes. The visual depictions of the land in the maps and the cover-art bring to life the vivid descriptions of Middle-earth in the writing itself. These descriptions are further enhanced by the art from his other works, *The Hobbit* and *The Silmarillion*.

Tolkien believed in the heroic quest or journey as one of growth by overcoming natural and human-made obstacles. His landscape forms—the settled Shire, dark caves, towers of evil, and forests of mystery—were devised with the purpose of testing the characters' resolve and teaching them. The land in Middle-earth, although corrupted in parts, was inherently good, and Tolkien represented a closeness to land and nature as a positive character trait. Further, he celebrated the act of venturing outwards onto the road, and the bravery of merely embarking on a journey. For Tolkien, the physical journey mirrored the hero's journey his characters undertook, embodying courage, hope, and eventual redemption.

As readers, we take away lessons. The land around us is deeply historical, with the current state of it just the latest manifestation. Spirits and spirit fill the natural world; the land has the potential for good and evil. Industry corrupts the land, and there is a pastoral pre-industrial optimum (represented by his depiction of the Shire) that is an ideal to strive for. As we read, we can put ourselves in the shoes of the main characters. Early on, Frodo takes on an alias and puts forth that he is writing a book on history and geography. This is exactly the role Tolkien himself plays, offering us a history and depiction of the land. Like Frodo, it is our job to venture out into the world, push ourselves beyond boundaries, and explore, learn, and understand. In the end, it is the role of the characters (and by implication, our mission too) to redeem the land, repair its hurts, and restore it to goodness. In this, Tolkien was, in a sense, an early environmentalist.

After the publication of LOTR, Tolkien wrote a reader, "I wisely started with a map and made the story fit." Tolkien's vision of the landscape and the themes he expresses are worth our consideration: he saw meaning in the land, and in his story, expresses a viewpoint about the land for the reader to take away. We can look at the value he placed on English countryside forms in his description of the Shire, his view of wild lands, his sense of landscape history, his conception of good and evil in the land, and his belief in redemption. We will explore these themes in the Essais below, and I thank you for your forbearance as I geek out on this fantasy world.

Although one continuous story, for publishing ease Tolkien split The Lord of the Rings *into six parts split across three separate volumes:* The Fellowship of the Ring, The Two Towers, *and* The Return of the King.

ESSAI 18
Tolkien…The Shire

In one of his first jobs after university and after his service in World War I, J.R.R. Tolkien worked on the development of the original *Oxford English Dictionary*. The OED was a monumental effort in philology, eventually comprising 400,000 English word definitions across ten volumes, published between 1884 and 1928. More than just definitions, the OED is a history of words from their pre-modern language derivations to examples of their usage through time to the present. Tolkien only worked on the OED for two years before becoming a junior professor at the University of Leeds. Still, of his experience at OED he wrote later that he "learned more in those two years than in any other equal period of my life."

He certainly did, and throughout his descriptions in *The Lord of the Rings*, Tolkien shows love for words and precision in word choice to both portray a scene and set a tone. In his descriptions of the Shire, Tolkien writes of thickets, coppices, tussocks, dells, brambles, and hedges, as he creates a picture of the Shire reminiscent of the 19th-century English countryside. He later writes of barrows, dikes, crags, towers, coombs, holds, and meres when he describes older landscapes often with crumbling ruins. In describing valleys or depressions in the land, Tolkien uses a variety of words: vale, dale, fosse, dingle, dell, ghyll, and hollow. The flora he cites include hedgerows, briars, swards, launds, and copses, not to mention trees of many types. Towards the end of LOTR, he describes the Pelennor Fields near the fortress city of Minas Tirith as follows: "The townlands were rich, with wide tilth and many orchards, and homesteads there were with oast and garner, fold and byre, and many rills rippling through the green from the highlands." Here, he seems to draw on more medieval words to describe the countryside around the castle-like city. And despite our not quite knowing these words, we understand the tone and the overall meaning (for reference: tilth=tilled lands; oast=a drying shed or barn; garner=granary; fold=sheep pen; byre=cow house; rill= small brook).

From ages 4 through 8, Tolkien lived in the English village of Sarehole, a small hamlet in Warwickshire, southeast of but very near the growing industrial city of Birmingham. Sarehole was idyllic with a mill and millpond, swans, fields, a dell with flowers and woods, and surrounding farms. It was this childhood memory that provided the template for his literary landscape of the Shire. Tolkien's ideal sense of the land comprises the English Midlands of his childhood in the 1890s—a countryside still bucolic but adjacent to and slowly encroached on by the industrializing and modernizing world. Writing in 1964, Tolkien called out his "particular love of what you might call central Midland English countryside based on good water, stones and elm trees and small quiet rivers." The memory of Sarehole was made more poignant for Tolkien because at age 8, he moved to Birmingham, a burgeoning city which was then transforming from craft manufactures to large-scale metal-working industries.

Tolkien describes the Shire in the prologue of LOTR as "a well-ordered and well-farmed countryside." There are small villages like Hobbiton, Bywater, Tuckborough, Stock, and Buckleberry. There are fields, hedges, mills, woods, and copses.

The hobbits live in burrows in hillsides with round doors, circular windows, and small gardens—or in low-lying houses designed to resemble burrows. Tolkien created a watercolor painting for the cover-art of *The Fellowship of the Ring* that depicts his vision of the Shire near Frodo's and Bilbo's home of Bag End. In the foreground, we see a small brook turning a water-wheel mill constructed of local stone. There are low, thatched-roof buildings representing Hobbiton, with a nearby row of Chestnut trees. A road, lined by fences and hedges, extends up "The Hill," where it terminates at the front door of Bag End, the home of Frodo and Bilbo. We see tilled fields. We see other hobbit holes with their cottage gardens, and we see the garden of Bag End in front of its round windows, and nearby a small field with a big tree, which we will learn soon is the Party Tree where Bilbo gives his farewell speech.

It is clear from the cover art that the hobbits care for their land, as the fields and gardens are edged and clear of weeds, and the trees are well placed. Frodo states quite simply, "I love the Shire." The Shire is Frodo's and his friends' homeland, and the Hobbits care for the land imbues the Shire with a kind of power, which Gandalf notes stating, "there is a power in Rivendell to withstand the might of Mordor. There is power, too, of another kind in the Shire." Throughout *The Lord of the Rings*, Tolkien shows a close connection between the lands and the people who live there. The land takes on the character of the people. We see this later with the elf territory of Hollin. Though the Elves have departed, Hollin retains some sense of their magic in the holly trees and the magical door.

The Shire is pure, English countryside reflecting the simple, middling folk that the Hobbits are. There is a familiarity and a goodness to it. Tolkien uses the Shire as a base against which to draw contrast to other landscapes, both good and evil, that the hobbits journey through. What follows is a description of some of these different landscapes and their role in the story.

ESSAI 19
Tolkien...Kingdoms and Wilderland

Kingdoms

We learn quickly that the Shire is an island of rural settlement in a larger realm with its own deep history. In the Middle-Earth timeframe, the Shire is a new construct, having emerged only within the last 1,400 years. It is situated on land that used to be part of realm of Arnor, the northern kingdom of the men of the west. As part of that original kingdom, the Shire land was "well-tilled with many farms, cornlands, vineyards, and woods." The territory surrounding the Shire, however, is replete with ruins of the old realm. There are barrow tombs heaped by the "men of Carn Dum," old dikes (trenches) along the big east/west road, and a masonry ring of what was once an old tower on Weathertop Hill. On Weathertop, the Hobbits see "remains of green-grown walls and dikes, and in the clefts there still stood the ruins of old works of stone."

North of the Shire there once were the cities of Annuminas and Fornost, and south was the city of Tharbad. All are now in ruins; Fornost is referred to as "Deadman's Dike." Later in LOTR, we hear the southern kingdom of Gondor is also in decline. The city of Minas Tirith is "in truth falling year by year into decay; and already it lacked half the men that could have dwelt at ease there." Of the two other great cities of Gondor, Osgiliath is abandoned and now fought over territory. Minas Ithil has become evil, taken over by corrupt spirits, and is now named Minas Morgul, the Tower of Sorcery.

Tolkien creates this sense of a deeper past to enrich the novel and signal that something is wrong in this world. We wonder, What happened? The land outside the Shire is ruinous, overgrown, and unpeopled, whereas before there had been kingdoms. Tolkien reprises this idea in his descriptions of the abandoned Dwarf city of Dwarrowdelf. We learn of the Dwarf city, "of old it was not darksome, but full of light and splendour"—there was greatness that is now gone and abandoned to ruin.

We also learn of even more ancient times. Elves are abandoning Middle-earth, passing through the Shire to go to the havens to sail to the West. There are remnants of even earlier, pre-historic cultures in Tolkien's conception of the Woses, the wild men of the Druadan Forest, as well as ancient stone works and statues in the high dale of Dunharrow. Tolkien tells us that the carvings were "the work of long-forgotten men. Their name was lost and no song or legend remembered it." The lands of Middle-earth are layered with history, and we can still view the remnants. A key component of the novel will be about the transition from a bygone and declining older era to a new age and how the characters' actions bring this about. Middle-earth is a landscape in transition from ancient forms now ruined to modernity not yet constructed, and Tolkien's characters have a role to play.

Wilderland

In Tolkien's prequel to LOTR, *The Hobbit*, there is a map of the north part of Middle-earth labeled "Wilderland," and on the map is a double line labeled "Edge of the Wild." The Shire and the old kingdoms of men are on the west side of the line, while on the east side is a vast land comprised of abandoned highlands, the ominous Misty Mountains, the upper vale of the River Anduin, and the vast dark forest of Mirkwood. Tolkien demarcated this swath as "Wilderland" to signal that crossing into it was to leave the settled areas of towns and farms and head into more mysterious, challenging natural and wild landscapes.

In Tolkien's conception, Wilderland is not just a wild country, but contains an unconstrained nature. It is inhabited by beings with agency that test our hero characters. In *The Hobbit*, Bilbo journeys through Wilderland, encountering a succession of strange creatures: trolls and giants in the hills and mountains; elves in the valley of Rivendell and Mirkwood; goblins and wolves; giant talking eagles; large hissing spiders; and, a shape-changing bear-man named Beorn. The Wilderland is not a land of men, but an area where other creatures exist in a way to challenge Bilbo in his journey. Crossing the land itself requires climbing mountains, fleeing through caves, flying through the air, crossing a large river, and traveling for weeks in a seemingly endless forest. In *The Hobbit*, the land itself is a challenge to overcome.

Years later, Bilbo's past adventures through Wilderland are well-known by his young ward, Frodo. As Frodo approaches his middle age, the wild calls to him as it did to Bilbo, as he, "found himself wondering at times, especially in the autumn, about the wild lands and strange visions of mountains. ... [T]he old paths seemed too well-trodden. He looked at maps and wondered what lay beyond their edges." When Frodo takes up the quest to destroy the Ring, he finds the world outside the Shire is indeed wild. It is a place where it is easy to get lost. The hobbits and their companions need guides—first Tom Bombadil, then Aragorn, and much later Gollum—to assist them and lead them on the right paths.

Early on Frodo and his friends make their way through the Midgewater Marshes, which are bewildering and have "shifting paths and quagmires." Later, in their journey from Rivendell to the Misty Mountains, the wildness of nature seems to turn against them. First, vast flocks of crebain (crows) seem to be acting as spies, searching out the company at the behest of either the evil wizard Saruman or of the Dark Lord Sauron himself. They seek to cross the Misty Mountains by the Redhorn pass, but they cannot make it through the sudden snow storm that appears. The snow falls harder and faster as they move forward but lessens when they stop. Rocks fall on their path, and they hear "Fell voices on the air." "These stones are aimed at us," claims one of the travelers.

After retreating from snow and stones, the Fellowship finds itself surrounded by wolves. A nighttime battle breaks out. Legolas the elf slays many of the wolves, but, in the morning, none of the wolves' bodies can be found, only arrows on the ground. Crows, ghost-wolves, and the weather itself conspire against the Frodo and his companions. Evil purpose imbues the elements of nature. The Wilderland is not in the control of the hobbits or their companions—they are at odds with it. Nature in the Wilderland has agency and fights them. While the Shire is well-ordered, the Wilderland is disordered, anti-control, independent, and malevolent. Tolkien gives us a sense of how desperate the quest is, as the characters have to battle their way forward, with ongoing tests of courage.

ESSAI 20
Tolkien...Faerie Lands

Tolkien draws a series of sharp dichotomies in his depictions of landscape. First, he denotes the difference between inhabited lands like the Shire and abandoned lands—lands with ruins—like the old northern kingdom of Arnor. Tolkien then shows us the divide between areas of habitation and the true wilderness in Wilderland. There is a third type of land, though, which exists almost separately from Middle-earth, and that is the land of Elves—alternately called by Tolkien "Faerie"—which he shows us with his creations of the Old Forest, Rivendell, and most prominently with Lothlorien.

The hobbits encounter their first faerie land when they initially leave the Shire at the outset of their quest. Frodo and his friends are fleeing the Shire from pursuing Black Riders, agents of the enemy Sauron. Instead of traveling on the main east/west Road, they decide to take a shortcut through the Old Forest, despite its worrisome reputation. One of the hobbits tells Frodo, "But you won't have any luck in the Old Forest... You'll get lost. People don't go in there."

The hobbits kick off their journey by cutting through the giant hedge that protects that portion of the Shire from the Old Forest. As they initially make their way in the woods, it becomes clear that it is suffused with a spirit and intent. Merry tells us, "Everything in [the Old Forest] is very much alive, more aware of what is going on…than things in the Shire. And the trees do not like strangers. They watch you… the most unfriendly ones may drop a branch or stick a root out with a long trailer." The hobbits feel "the ill will of the wood pressing on them." It is stuffy and warm in the woods. The trees seem to move and creak and press in on them, shunting the Hobbits from their intended direction and pushing them south toward the Withywindle River valley, which we learn is "the queerest part of the whole wood, the centre from which all the queerness comes."

Even at the outset of their journey, literally on day one, the Hobbits find themselves in a different world that is strange and filled with spirits. The hobbits become spellbound by the Old Man Willow tree and are trapped in its roots, only to be rescued by Tom Bombadil with his unique magic. Tom Bombadil and his wife Goldberry are nature fairies who tap into the power of the natural world through verse and song. Goldberry herself is called out as the daughter of the river.

With the Old Forest, Tolkien has immediately immersed his characters (and us readers) in a land where the normal rules do not apply. We find that a willow tree has evil intent. Tom Bombadil can sing songs and manipulate flora and fauna. The Forest has a different magical feel. This is not like the Shire farmland, nor is it like the Wilderland where more normal physics of nature apply. The Old Forest is magical, and the role it plays is to challenge the Hobbits stay on course, make it through, survive, and learn.

We see this idea of a magical, faerie landscape again with the land of Rivendell. Rivendell is the home of Elrond, the half-elven, who is a scion of both ancient human and elf lineage. Rivendell is a valley, and Elrond's home is called "The Last Homely House." The house is large, with many rooms, porches, and gardens, but, importantly, neither the house nor

Rivendell is a fortified castle or land. Rivendell is a natural valley, a sward of green lawns, trees, and a small river, set amidst otherwise barren land. The air in the valley is warmer, and there is a magical, healing feel. Travelers recoup there after long journeys. Later in LOTR, we learn that Elrond has one of the three Elven Rings, which he uses to imbue the valley with healing power. Tolkien writes, "...such was the virtue of the land of Rivendell that soon all fear and anxiety was lifted from their minds. The future, good or ill, was not forgotten, but ceased to have any power over the present." The passage of time and attendant anxieties fade in Rivendell. The Hobbits are "content with each good day as it came, taking pleasure in every meal, and in every word and song." The healing and almost time-stopping magic of Rivendell's valley enabled the Hobbits and the other inhabitants to live both fully aware of their lives and selves while also free from immediate fear. In Rivendell, the Fellowship of the Ring forms as Frodo and his companions commit to the quest to destroy the Ring of Power. Rivendell is a cynosure of rest and gathering, but also clarity and purpose against the great evil.

We see similar magic, but even more so, when the Fellowship, after many hardships, arrives later at Lothlorien, another Elvish land. Similar to the Old Forest and Rivendell, Lothlorien is a natural setting. It is not a place of dikes, battlements, or castles. The Elves in Lothlorien live in trees. Two rivers, Anduin and Celebrant, guard the heart of the land. Nature is untouched by artifice and has a strange atmosphere. As Frodo crossed the river into Lothlorien, "It seemed to him that he had stepped over a bridge of time into a corner of the Elder Days, and was now walking in a world that was no more." The moribund outside world recedes, and the group has entered, again, into a world of magic: "A light was upon it for which his language had no name. All that he saw was shapely, but the shapes seemed at once clear cut, as if they had first been conceived and drawn at the uncovering of his eyes, and ancient as if they had endured forever."

Lothlorien is a counterpoint to the forsaken moors, snowy mountains, and dark caves the group had just endured. There are no trees like the Mallorn trees they see in Lothlorien, as the leaves do not fall in autumn, but turn gold and stay on the limb until spring when new flowers emerge. The leaves are golden, and the tree trunks are silver. Despite the winter, there are flowers and green grass. It is a beautiful world, with magical flora, that feels pure, original, and untouched. The vicissitudes of weather and time are kept at bay; in fact, after eventually leaving Lothlorien, Frodo and his companions have lost track of time, not realizing they have spent a full month there.

The magic in Lothlorien comes from the elf queen Galadriel who, like Elrond, has a magic ring. Her ring is Nenya, the Ring of Adamant. This name reflects Galadriel's adamantine stance against the Dark Lord and her determination to retain in Lothlorien the spirit and feeling of past ages.

As with all the faerie realms in LOTR, Lothlorien is not just a respite on the journey but also demands added strength from its characters. In the Old Forest, the hobbits had to brave the unknown, confront evil in Old Man Willow, and experience wonder at the magic of Tom Bombadil. In Rivendell, Frodo had to make the personal commitment to destroy the Ring and undertake with the Fellowship the arduous quest to Mount Doom. Lothlorien is equally challenging to our heroes, but less physically and more spiritually. During their stay there, Galadriel confronts each of the characters with a choice of whether to go on with the quest or turn away, having them face their fears and desires. Galadriel showed Sam, for example, the chance of "flying back home to the Shire to a nice little hole— with a bit of garden of my own." In experiencing Galadriel's challenges, each character must renew his commitment to the quest and summon further courage. The experience strengthens their resolve, and the Fellowship emerges from Lothlorien rested and restored physically, but also, for most of them, psychically. The faerie lands are designed for passing through, less an escape from the world, and more a spiritual test on a hero's journey.

ESSAI 21
Tolkien...Evil and Caves

A great benefit of fantasy literature is the ability to denote good and evil, often with little nuance or ambivalence. With fantasy characters, we have heroes and foes, and sometimes heroes who fall into evil and evil characters who are later redeemed. In LOTR, for example, we see this with the character Gollum, who begins as a hobbit-like character named Smeagol, but falls into evil when he steals the Ring from his neighbor Deagol. The Ring then further corrupts Gollum: he hisses; he talks to himself in the third person; he lives in a cave; his skin is gray-hued and slimy; he cannot abide the sun; and he murders (often). There is an evil clarity to the character of Gollum. Even when he tries to redeem himself, he is either acting fully one way (loyal and fawning to Frodo) or entirely another (malevolently scheming to kill Frodo and Sam).

Similarly, in the landscapes he creates, Tolkien denotes good lands and evil lands, clearly delineating both. Good lands, like the Shire or Lothlorien, have a purity and naturalness, with the inhabitants having an affinity to their locale. Evil areas become evil through abandonment, neglect, lawlessness, or pollution. The worst places, though, are possessed with evil spirits, haunted with a malice that imparts an even more sinister character.

Tolkien is clear throughout all of his work that land and nature do not start as evil, but that neglect or lack of stewardship can trigger decay. We've discussed the abandonment and ruin of the northern kingdom of Arnor. There is lawlessness in the north that forces the small pockets of development—like the Shire, Buckland, or Bree—to be fenced and defended. The Shire at the outset of LOTR has had to increase border patrols—the Shirrifs—because of intrusions and weird occurrences. Outside the Shire, Aragorn's Rangers make a special effort to defend the Shire and other scattered communities as well. Both Buckland and Bree have surrounded themselves with huge hedges and guarded gates to fence out strangers and retain their lands. Much later, we see that the men of Minas Tirith have built a wall around their townlands—the "Rammas Echor"—because of the need to defend their settlements. In a world that is descending into evil, walls become necessary. Even the Elven Rivendell and Lothlorien rely more and more on their river barriers and the magic in those rivers for a first-line defense.

Frodo and Sam see further corruption of the land as they approach Mordor. After they leave their friends at the Falls of Rauros, Frodo and Sam begin journeying through a truly forsaken world. First, they traverse a hilly, denuded upland called the Emyn Muil, a place with no plants or trees and whose craggy hills and ravines make progress for the two hobbits difficult. Frodo and Sam, now with Gollum as a guide, then descend from the hills to make their way through the Dead Marshes: "Mists curled and smoked from dark and noisome pools. The reek of them hung stifling in the still air. The only green was the scum of living weeds on the dark greasy surfaces of the sullen waters." Truly horrific, the Dead Marshes are lands corrupted by the deaths of people who battled there long ago, and whose ghosts can still be seen in the ponds and muck.

The next stage of the journey takes Frodo, Sam, and Gollum across the Battle Plain, which leads to the Black Gate of Mordor, where the enemy Sauron has his kingdom. Of the

Battle Plain, Tolkien writes: "Here nothing lived, not even the leprous growths that feed on rottenness. The gasping pools were choked with ash and crawling muds, sickly white and grey, as if the mountains had vomited the filth of their entrails upon the lands about.... [G]reat cones of earth fire-blasted and poison-stained, stood like an obscene graveyard in endless rows."

Here, Tolkien likely draws on his own experience on the front lines in World War I. He suggests that lands, where vast numbers of people have died in battle, are permanently scarred and perhaps uninhabitable. As the action moves closer to Sauron and his kingdom, the lands become more and more evil. The malice of the Dark Lord Sauron corrupts the earth, erasing natural elements and leaving desert and dust. This evil land serves as a trial for Frodo. Biblically, the journey represents his 40 days in the desert, steeling his intent and determination before the final sacrificial push into the dark land itself.

Caves

We confront an even deeper evil when Tolkien's characters venture into caves and underground passages. These journeys into and through the darkness become the ultimate heroic test for key characters, as they must overcome fear and even death. Although there are beautiful caves, like the Glittering Caves of Aglarond beloved by Gimli the dwarf, uncorrupted natural caverns are outliers in Middle-earth. The former underground dwarf city of Dwarrowdelf is now called more ominously the Mines of Moria. Long ago, the dwarfs delved too deep and awakened a malevolently fiery being, a Balrog, who destroyed the dwarfs and their city. Moria is now dark and perilous, with the presence of the Balrog and also infested now by orcs. Our heroes only survive through Gandalf's sacrifice, as he defends a bridge as they flee.

Later, Aragorn and his company must travel the "Paths of the Dead," a trip through a long, dark cavern underneath the haunted mountain Dwimmorberg. In the cavern, they encounter a ghost army, which engenders great dread and fear, and which Aragorn must master to proceed on his quest. Similarly, Frodo and Sam have to travel through a long tunnel and cave to enter Mordor in their quest to destroy the Ring. There they encounter the giant spider-beast Shelob, who for eons has been trapping and killing creatures of all kind.

In all three instances, these caves require the utmost courage to enter. Choosing to go through the caves is an act of desperation when there are no other options. The Fellowship must travel through Moria because the mountain passes are snowed in, and wolves are pursuing them. Aragorn and his company perforce take the Paths of the Dead to make it to the ship landings at Pelargir in time to stop the enemy fleet. And, for Frodo and Sam, the cave of Shelob is the path into Mordor that seems least guarded by Sauron or his minions.

After summoning the courage to go underground, our hero characters experience something much worse than initially thought possible. For the Fellowship in the Mines of Moria, it is the fall of Gandalf into the crevasse and their belief that he has now died. For Aragorn and his company, it is the confrontation with the ghost army with the ultimate fear of death as experienced and narrated by Gimli. And, for Frodo and Sam, it is the believed killing of Frodo from the sting of Shelob. Deep in the earth, our characters find death, and from this confrontation, they summon a more profound strength to persist and continue despite fear and heartbreak.

The contrast between darkness and death in the caves and the goodness and strength of the light outside is a theme throughout LOTR. Each character confronts a darkness of evil creatures and potential death by bringing light into the cavern.

Gandalf's staff lights the way for the Fellowship through Moria. Aragorn brings torches into the Dwimmorberg. Frodo fights Shelob less with his sword, but by bringing light into the cave via a magic lamp, the Phial of Galadriel. The light bursts forth and burns the eyes of the evil Shelob. This active fight with darkness is later seen on an even larger scale as Mordor's darkness covers the entire land as a prelude to battle. A cloud of smoke from Mount Doom's volcano in Mordor extends out and shrouds the land of Gondor. It is only with the coming of a breeze from the south that the overcast dissipates, and Aragorn can sail from Pelargir and save the city on Minas Tirith.

ESSAI 22
Tolkien...Towers and Mordor

Towers

In the second and third volumes of LOTR, the great drama of the War of the Ring plays out amidst high castles with their mighty towers. Whether it is Saruman's Orthanc, Sauron's Barad-dur, the great citadel of Minas Tirith, or the haunted Minas Morgul, towers are cynosures of action where battles take place, but also giant, watchful sentinels to be avoided. Tolkien projects an ambivalence about these imposing structures, as they are both symbols of necessary strength and emblems of pride to be overcome.

From the top of a tower, one can see long distances and decry what is going on. The tower of the Dark Lord, Barradur, in Mordor seems to have a giant, evil eye peering forth searching the land, trying to find Frodo and the Ring. Another evil tower, on the borders of Mordor, Minas Morgul, has been possessed by evil spirits, the Nazgul, who have corrupted the tower and keep watch on the surrounding valley. Tolkien describes Minas Morgul as, "Paler indeed than the moon ailing in some slow eclipse was the light of it now, wavering and blowing like a noisome exhalation of decay, a corpse-light, a light that illuminated nothing." The flowers of the valley where the tower sat were "beautiful and yet horrible of shape, like the demented forms in an uneasy dream; and they gave forth a sickening charnel smell." Minas Morgul kept watch over the valley to deter intrusion while poisoning the land itself with its malice.

Minas Morgul's sister tower is Minas Tirith, the capital city and citadel of the southern kingdom of Gondor. This tower was a bastion against Minas Morgul's evil and indeed all of Mordor, but is corrupted too in its own way. The leader of Gondor, the Steward Denethor, would sit in the tower and use a magic stone to see what was going on around his lands. In doing so, though, he was entrapped by the Sauron's will and forced to see images of enemy armies, fire, and death, leading to despair. All those in towers, including Saruman in his tower of Orthanc, become ensnared by the enemy and turned to evil.

Towers manifest pride and ego. They are a testament to power, used by rulers to dominate the surrounding land, an expression of force over the landscape, reflecting a lack of humility in the builders. In LOTR, towers are egoic traps, and Tolkien draws a contrast to other structures. The hobbit buildings are humble, low structures resembling burrows close to the ground. Despite Elrond's high lineage, his abode in Rivendell is just a house—The Last Homely House—not a castle or tower. Even Galadriel, who has a history of being prideful and vies with Sauron in an ongoing test of mental will, still lives in a house in a tree, albeit a large one.

Towers and high places, in general, are fraught. When he foolishly sat in the chair on top of the Hill of Seeing (Amon Hen), Frodo was almost spotted by the eye of Sauron: Frodo "suddenly felt the Eye. There was an eye in the Dark Tower that did not sleep.... It leaped towards him; almost like a finger he felt it searching for him." In the end, we see that all of the lords of towers come to a bad end. It is the little, close-to-the-ground, humble hobbits, Frodo and Sam, who, hiding in dells, hollows, and ravines, are able to slip by the towers' eyes and make it to Mount Doom to destroy the Ring.

Mordor

The most evil land of all is Mordor, the kingdom of Sauron. Mordor is in the southeast of Middle-earth, across the river Anduin from Gondor and Minas Tirith. It is a dark land, under a perpetual cloud from the smoke spewing from the volcano Mount Doom. Two mountain ranges border Mordor: the Ephel Duath (Mountains of Shadow) and the Ered Lithui (Mountains of Ash). The two ranges meet at Cirith Gorgor, the Black Gate, which is approached from outside via the Battle Plain. Embraced by the arms of these ranges is the plain of Gorgoroth, an arid desert which includes Sauron's fortress of Barrad-dur and the volcano, Mount Doom. The name "Gorgoroth" is perhaps reminiscent of the word Golgotha, the biblical "place of skulls," where Jesus was crucified. Just as Jesus had to go through his trials in Golgotha, we see Frodo similarly carrying the Ring, his cross, on a journey of anguish and sacrifice across Gorgoroth. Indeed the journey culminates with the climb up Mount Doom with an ever heavier Ring, evoking Jesus's trial on Calvary.

Tolkien pulls no punches in his description of the corruption of nature in this horrid land: "...coarse grey grass-tussocks fought with the stones, and withered moss crawled on them; and everywhere great writhing, tangled brambles sprawled. Some had long, stabbing thorns, some hooked barbs that rent like knives....their maggot-ridden buds were just opening. ... [A]ll seemed ruinous and dead, a desert burned and choked." And of Mount Doom, Tolkien writes, "the light of [its flames] glared against the stark rock faces, so that they seemed to be drenched with blood."

The landscape is not just dead, it is murderous; and indeed, Frodo's and Sam's journey across Mordor slowly destroys them. They understand that they will not survive, that they will run out of food and water and not be able to escape back out of the dark land. Yet, they go on, not with hope for themselves, but with a simple understanding of the job they have to do.

In the end, Frodo and Sam complete the quest and destroy the Ring, and here we see what happens to the land when a great evil departs: "Towers fell and mountains slid; walls crumbled and melted, crashing down; vast spires of smoke and spouting steams went billowing up, up until they toppled like an overwhelming wave... The skies burst into thunder seared with lightning. Down like lashing whips fell a torrent of black rain." Also, "the creatures of Sauron, orc or troll or beast spell-enslaved, ran hither and tither mindless; and some slew themselves, or cast themselves in pits, or fled wailing back to hide in holes...." Without Sauron's evil power, the land crumbles, the Black Tower falls, and his slaves lose their purpose. We understand that Mordor is topography pasted together via Sauron's malice, but which then seismically falls apart once that interstitial evil is overcome.

ESSAI 23
Tolkien...Gardeners and Healers

If one of the roles, or outcomes, of the actions of Sauron and his minions is to destroy the land, marking it as evil and uninhabitable, the role of our hero characters must be one of restoration. In LOTR, Tolkien shows characters' devotion to fixing their world by bringing back flowers, plants, and trees, repopulating the landscape, and bringing a new order to the countryside. Further, Tolkien shows how restoration can bring a sense of holiness back to the landscape. So let's look at some of the key characters in LOTR and the role they play.

Hobbits are the best-known creation of Tolkien, and he purposefully devised them as creatures close to nature. They live in the land, in burrows in the ground. They physically touch the land, as they do not wear shoes, but have hairy feet. Hobbits have "a close friendship with the earth." They can move quietly through the land, barely disturbing plants and animals. Early on, as Frodo, Sam, and Pippin leave Hobbiton, they decide to cut across the country. They, "...took to the fields, passing into darkness like a rustle in the grasses. ... Even the wild things in the fields and woods hardly noticed their passing." It is this closeness to the land and their diminutive stature that enables their accomplishments.

Tolkien draws the contrast between these tiny folk and the larger world around them and the great deeds they undertake.

Frodo, with humility, saw himself as "a little hafling from the Sire, a simple Hobbit of the quiet countryside, expected to find a way where the great ones could not go, or dared not go." Pippin thinks of himself as "one small soldier in a city preparing for a great assault." Merry was "borne down by the insupportable weight of Middle-earth. He longed to shut out the immensity...." And Sam "knew in the core of his heart that he was not large enough... The one small garden of a free gardener was all his need and due." The hobbits are humble, sized for gardens and small fields, not for castles and mountains. While Tolkien plays out the vast action in his story across realms, rivers, and plains, the true heroism occurs down near the ground. Frodo and Sam hide in small dells. Merry crawls across the ground to stab upward into the knee of the Lord of the Nazgul. Pippin does the same with a giant troll.

Gimli the dwarf was one of Frodo's eight companions that set out on the quest to destroy the Ring. In Tolkien's conception, dwarfs are shapers of stone, delving huge caverns and making them beautiful, mining for ore and gems to grow their wealth and make beautiful things. The presumption is that dwarfs must be anti-nature, that in contrast to hobbits or elves they could be destructors of the natural world. Yet, this is not true. In speaking of the Glittering Caves of Aglarond, Gimli says of his people: "None of Durin's race would mine those caves for stone or ore... Do you cut down groves of blossoming trees in the springtime for firewood? We would tend these glades of flowering stone, not quarry them." Gimli sees his role as that of an artisan, who with a sensitivity to his material, takes natural forms and makes them more beautiful and useful. Despite his grim mien and the bluntness of his language, Gimli has an aesthetic appreciation that manifests in how he views the world. His love for the beauty of Galadriel is a testament to his sentiment.

Gimli›s closest friend in the Fellowship is Legolas the elf from the woodland kingdom in Mirkwood. Similar to Tom Bombadil and Goldberry, Legolas has an affinity to nature, especially trees and forests. He moves through nature with seeming effortlessness, running across snow without leaving a footprint. He sees far across the land, espying details and using his vision as a bowman par exemplar. Legolas and Gimli have an ongoing repartee, with Gimli advocating stones and caverns and Legolas trees and forests. When they are in Minas Tirith, in the midst of war, both have an eye to how they can make the city better in the future. Gimli studies the city: "There is some good stone-work here ... but also some that is less good and the streets could be better contrived. ... I shall offer [Aragorn] the service of the stonewrights of the Mountain." Legolas replies, "They need more gardens. ... The houses are dead, and there is too little here that grows and is glad. ... [T]he people of the Wood shall bring him birds that sing and trees that do not die." Gimli and Legolas both bring something to the table, and Tolkien sees the benefit of both the artisan and the gardener. Neither desolate stone nor unbounded forest is appropriate going forward in Middle-earth. And, both Gimli and Legolas have an intent to fix and heal the city of Minas Tirith, a theme we shall return to.

Perhaps the most fantastical creatures of Tolkien's invention are the Ents—-the "Onodrim." The Ents are tall, tree-like creatures who live in Fangorn Forest. They are shepherds of trees and have grown to look like trees themselves, and each bears the name of the tree species they resemble. Ents are devoted to maintaining their forest and saving the trees nearby and within, and as such, they see orcs and later Saruman as enemies because of their wanton hewing and destruction.

Like elves, Ents are immortal, and long ago, there were Entwives from which the Ents are now estranged. Ents manifest nature as unadulterated and original: "the Ents loved the great trees, and the wild woods, and the slopes of the high hills; and they drank of the mountain-streams, and ate only such fruit as the trees let fall in their paths." The chief Ent, Treebeard, does not have a constructed hall or home but just a mountain-cleft lined with evergreens. He spends his day walking with long strides through his forest, talking to tree friends.

Treebeard, in his conversation with Pippin and Merry, questioned them about the Shire because he thought it the kind of place where the lost Entwives might live. Treebeard tells them that the Entwives desired order in the land; they wished nature to hear and obey their wishes and grow and "bear leaf and fruit to their liking." The Entwives were agricultural, planning gardens and tilling land. This led to an estrangement between the tree-loving Ents and the Entwives. The Ents are endangered; there are only male Ents and no "Entings."

In Tolkien's conception, the male Ents had a failed strategy: they did not adapt to agricultural life. Ents still live in and value a pre-farming, undeveloped world. As we look to Ents and elves, we see two races of immortal beings, but also two races whose conception of nature as preserved and untouched will not survive in the Middle-earth of the future. Indeed, as the Fourth Age begins after the fall of Sauron, it will now be the time of men (and to a lesser extent hobbits) to thrive and expand. Ents and elves will leave Middle-earth, or die out, and the pastoral, agricultural nature of men and hobbits, not the wild forests, will become the norm.

ESSAI 24
Tolkien...Redemption

Nearly all of the heroic characters in LOTR take on an added role beyond the primary quest to destroy the Ring and eliminate the legions of the Dark Lord. After the destruction of their enemies, it is the role of the victors to now heal the land from its wounds. Areas that were once good have become corrupted during the occupation by the enemy, and it is not enough that the enemy be expelled from their lands. The land must be returned to goodness, remade into a garden or into a pastoral landscape imbued with positive aesthetic and spiritual qualities. By depicting these actions, Tolkien suggests that it is our role too to be stewards of goodness in the landscape, and that the task of caring for the land has a heroism equal to the actual achievement of the quest. It is not just enough to overcome evil. One must rebuild too.

We see this idea in the land of Ithilien. Ithilien was once known as "the garden of Gondor." Ithilien lies between the river Anduin and the Mountains of Shadow and was "a fair country of climbing woods and swift-falling streams." There were "a wealth of sweet smelling herbs and shrubs," and "many great trees grew there." However, because of its closeness to Mordor, the land had become marred by servants of Sauron. Frodo and Sam find "a pit of uncovered filth and refuse, trees hewn down wantonly and left to die," "a ring still scorched by fires," and "a pile of charred broken bones and skulls." The orcs not only perpetrate evil by murdering people, cutting down trees, and leaving open pits, but they seem almost intent to leave the land permanently scarred by their actions. The trees are cut down for no purpose. The refuse and bones are left unburied. Monuments are knocked over. We see a land that is en route to corruption, the darkness of Mordor extending outwards.

We see a similar corruption, but on an even larger scale with Saruman's intent and effect on the valley of Isengard. We hear from Gandalf that Isengard had once been "green and fair," but Saruman has filled it with "pits and forges" with dark smoke hanging over everything. Treebeard, the leader of the Ents, later tells us that Saruman "is plotting to become a Power. He has a mind of metal and wheels; and he does not care for growing things. ... Down on the borders they are felling trees—good trees. Some trees they just cut down and leave to rot ... but most are hewn up and carried off to feed the fires of Orthanc. There is always smoke rising from Isengard these days." The valley of Isengard, which had once had groves of trees, has become full of weeds, thorns, and "rank grass." We learn, "Shafts were driven deep into the ground: their upper ends were covered by low mounds and domes of stone so that in the moonlight the Ring of Isengard looked like a graveyard of the unquiet dead."

Saruman in his lust for power has created an evil, machine-filled land, exerting his selfish will, leading to the destruction of the environment (trees) to feed the fires of industry, and creating a rapacious ugliness. The growing industrial might of Isengard is corrupt in and of itself. There is smoke, and there even is rumor of a further corruption of nature as Saruman is creating a new race of orc, breeding orcs and men. Tolkien takes a stance here against the deprivations of nature inherent in industrialization and the aggrandizement of power.

We see this stance further with the descriptions of what is happening in the Shire with the mill at Hobbiton. First, in his depiction of the Shire, Tolkien highlights Hobbit industry as encompassing nothing more complicated than "a forge bellows, a water-mill, or a hand-loom." Yet when the Hobbits return to the Shire, after their quest, they find Sandyman's mill in Hobbiton replaced by a bigger one filled,

> ...*full 'o wheels and outlandish contraptions...[Ted Sandyman] works there cleaning wheels for the Men, where his dad was the Miller and his own master. ... They're always a-hammering and a-letting out a smoke and a stench, and there isn't no peace even at night in Hobbiton. And they pour out a filth on purpose; they've fouled all the lower Water, and it's getting down into the Brandywine. If they want to make the Shire into a desert, they're going the right way about it.*

An industrial mill has replaced the simple water mill of the past, and that intrusion of industry has made the former miller no longer a master of his craft, but just an employee of a company. We learn that this new mill was built not because there is more grain to grind, but to actually damage the Shire environment. We find out that Saruman is the mastermind behind the mill. He intends to mar the land by again introducing industry and attendant pollution, depleting natural resources. In his descriptions, Tolkien rejects this use of the land, and the new mill is eventually taken apart and then restored to its prior state.

So in LOTR we see a disparagement of industry and the industrializing world in favor of more straightforward landscapes of pastoral beauty and medieval errantry. Tolkien draws on his own life story where the blight of Birmingham where he lived in his teens contrasts with the ideal of the village of Sarehole where he lived when he was younger. Restoring landscapes requires bringing back the "garden," the ordered land of cottage plots of flowers and vegetables, tilled fields, and fenced husbandry.

One of the first acts of Aragorn, after he becomes king, is to appoint Faramir as Prince of Ithilien to go to that land with his new wife, Eowyn, and their followers to re-establish occupancy and order. After the Ents conquer Isengard and entrap Saruman, they immediately embark on restoring the beauty of the valley. The Ents first use the stream of the river Isen to flood the city, along with all of its pits and tunnels, to wash it clean of the dirt, grime, and pollution. They then finish tearing down the outer walls, so that the land around the Tower of Orthanc is re-opened. Once clean and open, "the land within was made into a garden filled with orchards and trees." Saruman's industrial landscape is gone, and the valley is remade into a pastoral entity with an ordered natural aesthetic. In a way, the Ents are now doing the work formerly attributed to the Entwives, planning and tilling Isengard with their orchards. Treebeard asks the hobbits once more before they leave to stay on the lookout for Entwives. With his husbandry Treebeard's hope springs eternal.

Similarly, Sam the Hobbit returns to the Shire and becomes the gardener of his land. The last chapters of LOTR—the trip into and through Mordor and the final return and redemption of the Shire—feature Sam as the primary hero character. It is through Sam's eyes and through his actions that much of the final drama plays out. And this is intentional. Although Frodo is 'The Ringbearer' and completes the quest, in his struggle he becomes a sacrificial figure. Frodo sacrifices his peace of mind when he destroys the Ring, suffers periodic bouts of pain, and retires quickly from the affairs of the world, eventually leaving Middle-earth entirely. That leaves Sam to play the role of land-redeemer, and it is in his role as gardener of the Shire where he has the most significant impact.

When the four hobbits return to the Shire after their long travels, they find the landscape transformed. Saruman and his men have enslaved much of the populace and have wreaked havoc on the land. The hobbits arrive at the Brandywine bridge to find a spiked gate, and two-story buildings with straight (not round) windows, "all very gloomy and un-Shirelike." Traveling across the land the next day, the hobbits noticed that "there was an unusual amount of burning going on." And, when they reached Hobbiton, beside the horror of the new mill, they saw, "Many of the houses they had known were missing. ... little gardens that used to run bright to the water's edge were rank with weeds. ... An avenue of trees had stood there. They all were gone. ... The banks and hedgerows were broken." Bagshot Row was dug up. The Party Tree was lying lopped and dead in the field. Sam noted, "This is worse than Mordor!" And for him it was: the destruction of the Shire was the same evil, but now it was more poignant since it was his homeland.

In the chapter titled "The Scouring of the Shire," we see how the Hobbits were able to kick ruffians out of the Shire and eliminate Saruman. As the word "scouring" connotes, Sam then led the Shire to clean out all of the filth, taking down the ugly houses and replanting trees and gardens. Sam has a magical gardening box that he received as a gift from Galadriel, and with the earth in that box he can fertilize new saplings that he planted so that they gained 20 years growth in just one. He also planted the nut of a Mallorn tree (the silver-trunked, golden-leaved tree of Lothlorien) to replace the Party Tree. The harms that the Shire suffered were fixed by Sam's hard work and leadership, unselfishly deploying his magic garden box, and encouraging the help of all the Shire folk.

Physical repair is accompanied by a spiritual awakening in the land. In the Shire, the magic earth from Sam's box does more than just incite growth, it actually creates an almost magical year of nascency with perfect weather, bumper crops, and beautiful children all born that year. When he tosses the final remnants of magic dust from his garden box in the air in the center of the Shire, Sam essentially baptizes and brings a sacredness to the land. In that special year of 1421, "there seemed something more: an air of richness and growth, and a glam of beauty beyond that of mortal summers."

Beyond just restoration, we see redemption and rebirth. Aragorn, now crowned King in Gondor, climbs with Gandalf up onto the mountain behind Minas Tirith, where they find a sapling of the White Tree. This tree is a descendant of an original tree of the Valar (the early gods of Middle-earth), and has been a symbol of the men of the west. Aragorn plants the tree, and it grows in the citadel garden of Minas Tirith, where it symbolizes rebirth, and indeed the finding of it heralds the marriage of Aragorn to Arwen. Both the planting of the Mallorn Tree in the Shire and the White Tree in Gondor echo the theme of Eden and its central tree. Sam and Aragorn are creating new Gardens of Eden imbued with a sacred orderliness that will allow for the flourishing of hobbits and men.

While Sam's profession is that of a gardener, Aragorn takes on the role of "healer" as part of his royal heritage. The conception of "king as healer" has roots in medieval notions of royal power. Even as late as the 18th century, the British Queen Anne would "lay hands" on petitioners who had sicknesses and wished for succor. Aragorn has the unique ability to use the plant Athelas to help those who are injured. The smell and essence of the plant, as Aragorn used it, seemed to summon a memory of naturalness and freshness. For some of the men it triggered "a keen wind … an air wholly fresh, clean and young … came new-made from the snowy mountains." While for Merry, the Athelas was, "…like the scent of orchards, and of heather in the sunshine full of bees." Nature, as represented by Athelas or Sam's garden box, is a healing tonic for the people of Middle-earth. It is a two way street: Tolkien is calling on us to be healers of the land, and in return nature's beneficence will heal us.

Peoples and lands that are truly blessed are those that are loved and treated with constant care, and it is in the quotidian care of our environment that the ultimate satisfaction can be found. Gandalf captures this sense of every-day heroism when he states, "It is not our part to master all the tides of the world, but to do what is in us for the succor of those years wherein we are set, uprooting the evil in the fields that we know, so that those who live after may have clean earth to till. What weather they shall have is not ours to rule."

ESSAI 25
Tolkien...The Road

For Tolkien, heroes manifest their courage through the simple act of taking to the Road, despite the uncertainties of their quest and the effect it may have on them. In LOTR, the word "Road" is always capitalized, and it occupies a place in the landscape and in the minds of his heroes equivalent to lands such as Gondor or the Shire or Rivendell. Going out on The Road and continuing forward, is the essence of the hero's quest, and Tolkien's imperative for his characters (and for us) is to take that step and venture out to learn, grow, and accomplish.

Early on in LOTR, Frodo feels a mental itch as he becomes older and confronts the sameness of his life; he, "looked at maps, and wondered what lay beyond their edges." Frodo knew his land of the Shire intimately: villages, mills, inns, farms, hedgerows, and coppice woods. But outside the Shire is mystery, and Frodo has a curiosity and desire to follow his uncle, Bilbo, but also a hesitancy to leave. He remembers the words of Bilbo: "there was only one Road...it was like a great river...its springs were at every doorstep, and every path was its tributary." "It's dangerous business ... going out your door. You step into the Road, and ... there is no knowing where you might be swept off to." For Frodo, the Road that leads down The Hill, where he lives, and into the village of Hobbiton is the same Road that crosses the Shire and leads through Bree, and circles around Weathertop on the way to Rivendell. And that same Road continues from Rivendell to Hollin, and Moria, and Isengard, and Rohan, and then further to Gondor and Mordor. Or in another direction, the Road travels over the Misty Mountains, across the Anduin, to Mirkwood and the Dwarf kingdom of Erebor .

Tolkien gives us a song about the Road that he reprises in different versions throughout LOTR. It goes like this:

The Road goes ever on and on
Down from the door where it began.
Now far ahead the Road has gone,
And I must follow, if I can,

Pursuing it with eager feet,
Until it joins some larger way
Where many paths and errands meet.
And whither then? I cannot say.

Here, Tolkien captures the mystery of what one may find on the Road while also noting compulsion we feel. The Road becomes a metaphor for life. Life starts at the doorstep now, and the adventure on the Road proceeds to an indeterminate future. The job of a person is to attempt the Road, the part of the Road he or she can see—positively, "pursuing it with eager feet." But this Road is not a straight line. It joins other roads and other purposes, and, in fact, we are not sure where this Road, this life, or even this afterlife is really heading.

Life is unexpected, and the quest that Frodo and his friends take is not pre-scripted, but contingent. Tolkien captures this sense of contingency in other versions of the song. One line goes, "Still round the corner there may wait; A new road or a secret gate." Another line calls out, "Still round the corner we may meet; A sudden tree of standing stone; That none have seen but we alone." Our own walks are this way, when we look around and see trees, or homes, or streets we may not have noticed before. We search for new things outside, and, in finding them, they become a secret uncovered that we have gained for ourselves. The Road becomes a critical mission for us to undertake. Yet another line from the song seeks to inspire: "Home is behind, the world ahead, And there are many paths to tread."

We see an ongoing commitment to the Road by the principal characters. Aragorn is known colloquially as "Strider" because he strides around the countryside, helping defend the land from the enemies. He tells us early on, "It is not my fate to sit in peace." Aragorn travels to many lands, and spends much of his early years on "errantry," searching for knightly adventure with the purpose of fighting evil. Gimli and Legolas join the Fellowship of the Ring despite the danger and despite the knowledge that their own homes will be facing battles without them. Elrond forewarned Pippin and Merry that they should not go on the quest, but should return to the Shire given potential challenges there. Pippin and Merry join the Fellowship anyway. The decision to go out on the Road is one of courage and hope despite the bad things that might occur to the homes they leave behind. In a way, these characters push all of their chips to the center of the poker table, because deep down they know that not to do so would entail loss for the world and for themselves.

We see this all-in approach further with Theoden, the King of Rohan. Once he is cured of his malaise by Gandalf ("Too long have you sat in the shadows and trusted to twisted tales and crooked promptings"), Theoden makes a series of choices to save his kingdom and eventually Gondor. First, he rises from the gloom of his chamber to step out into the sunlight of his terrace. He stands up "tall and straight" as he looks out over his kingdom. He then takes up his sword and goes out to battle, courageously heading towards the site where his son had been slain just a few days before. In battle, when all is despair, he chooses to make a charge with the men of his household on horseback, leading the way, despite overwhelming numbers of the enemy. After the battle is won, Theoden takes to the Road again, and confronts the evil wizard Saruman. He then sets out for Gondor to fight with his allies, despite knowing that an orc army has invaded the northern part of his kingdom.

Theoden's commitment to confronting the enemy is not quixotic, it is done with full knowledge of the high likelihood of his own death. Sam exemplifies this same trait in his support of Frodo on the quest. In Lothlorien, Sam re-commits to the Road, despite knowing that his father's home on Bagshot Row has been dug up. He continues on the Road through Mordor despite fast-dwindling water and food, and no real chance of returning alive. Sam thought,

> So that was the job I felt I had to do ... to help Mr. Frodo to the last step then die with him? ... But even as hope died in Sam, or seemed to die, it was turned to a new strength, as the will hardened in him, and he felt through his limbs a thrill ... that neither despair nor weariness nor endless barren miles could subdue.

The journey requires hope at first; but then when concern for oneself is no longer tenable, a new strength comes from self-abnegation. In a way, the confusion of the mind, as it vacillates between self-preservation and continuing forward, is clarified when the character gives up the ego, accepting death is perhaps imminent. The only choice is to proceed step by step to move forward on the Road.

The Road is thus an emblem of self-sacrifice. One heads

onto the Road for the quest, and, in doing so, one summons courage and hope, confronts evil, and undergoes a self-transformation sublimating one's ego for the larger purpose. Our characters are transformed, and we see this mostly with Frodo. Frodo's choice to take the Road was the choice to go on a long journey to his eventual death--a death that will come even despite his success in destroying the Ring. After they have returned to the Shire, Frodo explains to Sam, "I have been too deeply hurt ... I tried to save the Shire, and it has been saved, but not for me. ... when things are in danger, someone has to give them up, lose them so that others may keep them."

Frodo then takes to the Road one last time, when he travels to the Havens to take his final voyage and leave Middle-earth. In a final version of the Road song, we hear: "A day will come at last when I; Shall take the hidden paths that run; West of the Moon, East of the Sun." The final journey on the Road for Frodo (and for us), is the journey to death and potential afterlife. It is the ultimate sacrifice of friendships, family, and possessions, and the giving up of self.

The larger message we take away is that staying at home and self-involvement is never a good option. We must always choose to go out on the Road, even en route to our own final death. The quest does not end when just one thing is accomplished, no matter how epic, but always continues. It is our job to keep stepping out—"The Road goes ever on and on."

ESSAI 26
Heroes

The redeeming hero, the carrier of the shining blade, whose blow, whose touch, whose existence, will liberate the land.

—*Joseph Campbell*

No matter how banal our days, no matter how tedious our tasks, there exists within us a story of heroism. Inherent in life is authorship of personal destiny. Through time we learn and grow, struggle and sacrifice, succeed and even triumph. We begin life as egocentric, focused on ourselves, and our often petty wants and needs. But, over time, in school and at work, through hobbies and friendships, we gain in craft and knowledge and then put that expertise to use in creating new things for the betterment of family, community, and beyond.

Think for a bit about your life and what it took to get to the place where you are now. Reflect on the series of accomplishments and the times when you had to take on something new or work extra hard. Recognizing the heroic path we are on, building on what we have done, seeking new points of departure, journeying onto new roads into the unknown are the challenges we all have.

The best movies and books feature the "Hero's Journey," the archetypal story of self-realization through adventure, striving from the narrowness of current self-conception to eventual comprehension and succor of the wider world. The "Hero's Journey" was first defined by Joseph Campbell in his seminal work, *The Hero with a Thousand Faces*. Campbell writes of the "monomyth" where a reluctant hero senses a wrong to be righted. The nascent hero receives a call to adventure, and armed with advice from a mentor and often magical tools or weapons, heads forth from the familiarity of the quotidian to a new world of supernatural wonder. A long journey is undertaken through many lands. Allies join the quest. Seemingly insurmountable forces are encountered. The hero learns new knowledge and deeper empathy, growing spiritually through successive challenges. A final victory is won, and the hero returns transformed to the everyday world with a more accurate sense of self and the skills and power to lead and build her community.

We all know these stories, right? Young Luke Skywalker knows he wants something more than a life on barren Tatooine. A message from a princess comes to him, and he seeks the help of a wise old mentor, Ben Kenobi. Ben, aka Obi-Wan, advises and teaches Luke and gives him a special weapon—his father's light saber—and sets him on his path. After an initial refusal, Luke sets off on his quest to save the princess, gathering allies along the way—C3PO, R2D2, Han Solo, and Chewbacca. Luke enters the heart of enemy territory, the belly of the beast, the Death Star, and almost dies as he rescues Princess Leia. In the trash compactor on the Death Star, Luke finds himself confronting an actual beast when he gets pulled into the muck by a tentacled monster. In the end, though, Luke overcomes all challenges, destroying the Death Star and saving the rebellion.

Luke has further adventures in the subsequent films, eventually becoming a Jedi Master and fighting the evil Emperor Palpatine. In Luke, we see the need for physical strength and spiritual growth as he sacrifices himself for the rebellion. By the third movie, Luke has transformed from an impulsive boy with a simplistic desire for adventure to an almost-magical hero. Luke willingly sacrifices himself to save his friends, devoting himself to a higher purpose, ultimately redeeming his fallen father. In later movies, we see that Luke has become monk-like, no longer a physical fighter but spiritual, now training a new generation of Jedi.

So much of heroic literature captures the sense of journey. The hero seeks to break free from the sedentary and the mundane, and when the hero does burst forth from his old life into an adventure, he enters a landscape of challenge and wonder. Luke travels from his barren home planet to the metal Death Star, then to the ice planet of Hoth, and further to the jungles of Dagoba. The environments themselves trigger Luke's growth, especially his descent into the blackness of the cave on Dagoba. There, he confronts the darkness in himself in a vision of Darth Vader, who he later discovers is his father.

Heroic landscapes are wondrous, mind-opening, presenting problems and challenges for the hero. Heroic lands can be fanciful like those in "Star Wars," or Tolkien's Middle-earth, and there are many other examples. In C.S. Lewis's *The Lion, The Witch, and the Wardrobe*, the four Pevensie children play a child's game and hide in a wooden wardrobe. Emerging magically from the back of wardrobe, the children enter the wild world of Narnia where the witch queen and Aslan the Lion are enacting a classic battle of good versus evil across forests and mountains. Ursula LeGuin's fantasy world of Earthsea is an archipelago where people travel between islands, develop magical skills, and battle evil. Harry Potter's England has secret portals into hidden places like Diagon Alley and train platform 9 and 3/4. These stories are classic Bildungsromans where naifs like Harry, Ged, Frodo, and the Pevensies leave the everyday of their homes to experience challenges, tap into new powers, and grow into responsibility and purpose.

Other literary genres mirror these fantasy tropes. The English countryside of villages and farms has long been depicted as a place to escape from, or more often a place where local customs must be overcome. Anthony Trollope, Jane Austen, Emily Bronte, and Thomas Hardy all give us English heroes and heroines dealing with the embedded customs, and supposed ignorance, of rural England. Trollope himself was a postal inspector who traveled around southern England near Salisbury, where he found the inspiration for his *Chronicles of Barsetshire* novels. The Barsetshire books show the play of class and ambition brought down to the local village and county level, something Jane Austen specialized in as well. Emily Bronte found romance further north in the Yorkshire moors in *Wuthering Heights*, and indeed the landscape of moors and heaths as a setting of mystery and wild adventure crop up in other novels like Hardy's *Return of the Native*, Arthur Conan Doyle's *The Hounds of the Baskervilles* and Frances Hodgson Burnett's *The Secret Garden*.

Cities offer a different heroic prospect. With its long history of revolt and inherent sense of romance, Paris serves as the perfect backdrop for the novels of Victor Hugo and Honore de Balzac. Balzac especially seemed to revel in the diversity of the great city. More recently, New York has become a comedic setting in movies like "Home Alone II" and in the classic "When Harry Met Sally." In that film, Harry and Sally stroll in Central Park, drag a Christmas tree along a city sidewalk, and, in the end, Harry must run block after block to meet up with Sally and reconcile on New Year's Eve. Cities are, in their own way, fantastical and supply challenges for heroes. The Los Angeles of noir detective fiction with its seedy bars, down-and-out movie studios, and overriding feel of corruption provides the perfect setting for the hard-boiled, flawed detective hero.

And what is the Wild West of Louis Lamour or Zane Grey but a setting for character development, heroism, and love? The American West has allowed for the creation of a national mythos of good versus evil, the imposition of law onto chaos. With its vast plains, rivers, mountains, and deserts, the sheer size of the Western landscape becomes a force for characters to overcome. Larry McMurtry's novel *Lonesome Dove* features an epic journey from Texas to Montana. On the way, an old Texas Ranger, Gus McCall, must save Lorena, a prototypical damsel in distress. We see the tropes of Homer's *Odyssey* intermixed with medieval romance all played out on the Great Plains of North America.

Similarly, the Napoleonic seascapes of Patrick O›Brian›s Aubrey/Maturin novels and C.S. Forester›s Horatio Hornblower series allow for the same type of broad-scope drama and accomplishment. Pirate epics like *Treasure Island* or "Pirates of the Caribbean" are nothing more than Westerns set on the oceans. The wilds of Edgar Rice Burroughs' Africa in the Tarzan adventure novels or James Fenimore Cooper's Appalachia in the *Leatherstocking Tales* create adventure and growth for those heroes too. More recent children's books like *The Polar Express* and Philip Pullmann's *His Dark Materials* series leverage the icy north as a setting where characters confront adventure and danger. Similarly, we see war and battle scenes used as settings for heroic action: Virginia or Pennsylvania in Civil War novels like *The Red Badge of Courage* or *Killer Angels*; or the World War I trench scenes in novels such as Mark Helprin's *A Soldier of the Great War* or Erich Maria Remarque's *All Quiet on the Western Front*. Heroes amidst battle learn fear and courage, brotherhood and sacrifice, as well as the contingency and luck inherent in war.

Some lands serve a very different literary purpose. The pre-Civil war South is a landscape of strangeness and doom inherently corrupted by plantation culture. We see the old South as either falsely romanticized or something to escape from. *Gone with the Wind* seems (disturbingly) to celebrate the land, creating a false history of the South as if the plantation Tara is somehow a source of strength for the heroine Scarlett. *Huckleberry Finn* uses the areas bordering the Mississippi as a setting for absurdity and often death, which Huck and Jim must deal with. Autobiographical accounts like Solomon Northup's *Twelve Years a Slave* and Frederick Douglas's personal narratives detail the horror of the plantation landscape and the heroic effort to persist and escape. This sense of terror, conflict, and hypocrisy is captured fully in William Faulkner's Yoknapatawpha novels. We feel similar despair at lands depicted in recent World War II Holocaust novels and accounts, where sheer persistence is retold and given value in the face of the ultimate inhumanity. Concentration camps, slave plantations, and prisons serve to challenge the dignity and humanity of our heroes, who must both survive and help others while devising the eventual path to escape.

We celebrate heroes in novels and biographies, but I would argue that we are all playing out our existence in a heroic landscape, even if that is just our own homes, communities, workplaces, or schools. It is the conception of ourselves as the hero of our own lives that serves us best. I believe we must expand our awareness and elevate our sensibilities. We can become less reactive and more cognizant of how we play out our circumstances. We are nascent and filled with potential. Joseph Campbell writes:

> ...all the life potentialities that we never managed to bring to adult realization,

those other portions of ourself, are there; for such golden seeds do not die. If

only a portion of that lost totality could be dredged up into the light of day, we

should experience a marvelous expansion of our powers, a vivid renewal of life.

First we look around to see where we currently stand in the world. What is our home, our community, our job? We then think more broadly: what is it that we do not know that we want to explore?

The first step in any journey is to head out into the unknown, even if it is just in a small way. Whether the first step is intellectual, as simple as visiting a new bookstore section, or whether the initial attempt is physical, such as donning running shoes, perhaps, we can embark on an original path and begin our own growth. The journey is a moral one; it is about personal redemption, and through one's strife and victory comes a victory for others--family, friends, coworkers, and community. The journey is always difficult and will require sacrifice. But exploring new worlds, in the end, always helps us. The great news is that we can choose our significance, and in doing so, start the progress to our potentiality.

ESSAI 27
Trees

Keep a green tree in your heart, and perhaps a singing bird will come.

—Unknown

My children laugh at me because I'm a tree-hugger. I'm not a tree hugger in the usual sense of being an environmentalist trying to defend a tree from logging or as a spiritualist looking to reconnect with nature through somewhat off-putting physical contact (although I empathize with both thoughts). I am a tree hugger because I like to figure out how old trees are.

The best way to determine the age of a tree is not by hugging it but by determining the age of the home it fronts or the neighborhood in which it resides. Developers carved up empty fields for house lots, and tree-planting nearly always complemented the initial construction. If a house was built in 1933, and there is a large oak in front, then you can bet the tree is about 85 years old now. In my town, it is rare to find trees over 120 years of age. The Victorian houses of the 1890s have lost most of their original trees in the last 20 or so years. The streets with those 19th-century houses now have the appearance of new developments replete with many new-planted saplings and absent the expected large shade trees. Meanwhile, the homes built from the 1930s to the 1960s still sport majestic oaks, maples, or beeches, although I expect that many of these trees might be gone by mid-century as well.

Sometimes it isn't easy to gauge the age of a tree by its surroundings, which is where my tree hugging comes in. As trees age, they grow by adding successive rings around their trunks. Tree age is a function of its radius, or distance from the center of the trunk to its outer edge, reflecting the addition of rings each year. The actual size of those rings matters too. Although ring width varies based on the climate in a given year, on average, rings are consistent within a species over time. The location of a tree also plays a role, as I've found that the larger, older trees are often set back on a property. In contrast, those trees that line streets tend to grow more slowly and have a more limited lifespan perhaps because of the car pollution or, more likely, because root growth may be restricted.

To determine the total radius, i.e., measuring the sum of the width of all the rings from core to bark, we leverage our high school geometry by measuring the circumference of the tree and dividing by π to get the diameter (which is two times the radius). I hug trees to measure their circumference (and because let's admit it, it feels nice too) so I can figure out the radius and diameter, or the number of growth rings.

For the calculation, you will need to know what type of tree you are dealing with. As I'm driving, let's say I see a huge old oak tree in a side yard, and park the car. My arm span is about 6 feet, so I hug the tree at arm level above the ground (recommended) and find that the tree is right at 1.5 hugs or 9 feet in circumference, which is quite large. That is a circumference of 108 inches, which implies a radius of 17 inches and a diameter of 34 inches (remember diameter is circumference/π, and radius is half of the diameter). I then find the growth factor for that species of tree. You can find growth factors easily online, and the factor for most oaks is 4. Thus, a diameter of

34 inches times the growth factor of 4 suggests a tree that is 136 years old, which is pretty awesome. We should then look around to find an older house, or perhaps a barn, church, stone wall, inn, milepost, well, old mill, or village hall that somehow marked this tree as worth caring for over time.

My front yard is the home of two large trees. During a wind storm a few years ago, both trees lost several limbs, with one of the branches falling onto the power line for the house, leaving us without electricity. I spoke with the utility repairman, and he pointed out a problem with our two trees. He told me that the trees are not native to North America. He noted they are Asiatic Elms (there are several varieties), and, while they are pretty, their wood is somewhat soft, reflecting their more temperate climate heritage. He told me that Asiatic Elms do not stand up as well as native trees to the harsh climate of the U.S. Northeast and drop twigs and branches quite often.

There are several things to unpack here. First, I had never thought of the climate of the Northeast U.S. as that harsh. Still, I did some research and uncovered that my mid-Atlantic habitat is one of the world's worst climate areas. The Northeast suffers from extreme heat in the summer (as the weather travels directly over the West and Midwest United States, which heats the air) and extreme cold in the winter as the weather pattern shifts and drags polar air down from Canada. This is quite a contrast, for example, to the much more mild conditions of most of Europe. Even worse, the Northeast's proximity to the Atlantic allows for heavy rain and wind weather events to occur (the perennial Nor'easters). Periodically hurricanes or remnants of hurricanes or tropical storms also venture up the Atlantic coast bringing their own high winds.

What does this mean for trees in my area? Well, the wind often knocks them down. During Hurricane Sandy, we lost a group of 80-year-old Linden trees just a block away, which took several weeks to clear. My own elms have dropped huge limbs and require yearly trimming, at some expense. The original builders of my home planted the two trees in 1962 when they built the house, and they have grown to a beautiful expanse. But the question is, why did they plant these non-native trees? Why choose Asiatic Elms instead of the native American Elms, especially given how beautiful American Elm trees are? The answer has to do with beetles and a devastating ecological catastrophe.

In 1921 Europe underwent a new elm tree sickness identified initially in the Netherlands and labeled "Dutch Elm Disease." Essentially a fungus, "Ceratocystis ulmi," Dutch Elm disease spread rapidly through Europe via wind- and bird-borne spores. The disease reached the United States in 1930 via a shipment of elm logs imported from Europe for furniture construction. The fungus spread in the United States via bark beetles, and over the next 40 or so years, the American Elm species mostly died out in the United States.*

So many of our towns have Elm Streets, named when towns developed in the 19th century. Back in the day (the 1920s and earlier), American Elms with their vase-shaped upreaching limbs majestically bordered and shaded these roads. But now they are all gone. To see American Elms, one must find parks, or college campuses, where they can receive close care. American Elms still line and shade the famous "Mall" in Central Park, where landscapers carefully protect them from bark beetles and the disease.

Ancient, first-growth elms were stunning, large, with branches arcing upwards, creating a cathedral feel underneath. Their trunks were massive and gnarled, adding to the feeling of strength and persistence through time. The Deacon Elliot Elm on Boston Common became infamous during the Revolution as a gathering place for mobs to protest. Protesters hung British officials in effigy from the tree, made speeches, and roused rabble. Trees like the Deacon Eliot Elm became symbols of liberty during the Revolution, with a sense that freedom was rooted in American soil—that it was alive, vital, and continuous through time.

The idea of the "Liberty Tree" became part of the culture of protest throughout the colonies. Each town would designate a large, centrally located tree as its Liberty Tree. In Massachusetts, they were most often elms. Connecticut used oaks, Maryland tulips, and South Carolina live-oaks. People gathered at these trees on both ad hoc and formal occasions, including the signing of charters and forming new governments. Liberty Trees appeared on early state flags and coins. The trees also signified a threat to the British, with hanging as a form of retribution (a use that would horrifically manifest in lynching in later U.S. history).

Trees hold a place in our cultural history as spiritual symbols of freedom and strength, of persistence and renewal. In the mythic history of Robin Hood and his merry men, the characters wore green, hid in woods, and ambushed the rich by leaping out from trees. Celtic heritage included worshipping trees and tree gods and some early Christian groups still worshiped underneath ancient trees. The Garden of Eden featured two trees: the Tree of the Knowledge of Good and Evil and the Tree of Life. God expeled Adam and Eve from the Garden and thus from both true knowledge and eternal life. We now plant and celebrate symbolic trees as a recreation or memorial to the Garden. The cross of Jesus was often depicted as a palm tree; palm fronds are laid at Jesus's feet when he arrives at Jerusalem after 40 days in the desert. "Yggdrasil" is the tree of life in Nordic mythology and tradition. It represents the whole world and is often depicted as an ash or yew tree. The Buddha sat under the Bodhi tree to gain enlightenment.

Isaac Newton apocryphally discovered the law of gravity under an apple tree.

Thus, we see a long tradition of tree veneration, which is linked to thinking, contemplation, knowledge, and everlasting life itself. Trees create awe and instill within us a sense of history. They remain celebrated in our time as well, most notably with all of the Christmas trees, which call out the harvest, plenty, and celebration at the end of the year as well as the Christian symbolism of new life. Locally, we note and write about particular trees with an urgency to preserve history in the light of the ephemeral. On Long Island, there was the Big Oak, a famous tree that had reached 500 years in age, lasting from Columbus until, unfortunately, just a few years ago. In New York City, the Stuyvesant Pear Tree at 13th Street near Broadway provided a 200-year-old link between a modernizing New York and the small Dutch town it was in the 17th century. In my village, there is a local fight underway to preserve not just a historic Dutch heritage farmhouse, but the 200+ year old tree that stands alongside.

There is a saying that the best time to plant a tree is 20 years ago, which means, of course, that the best time to plant a tree is today. We all have learned the tremendous ecological efficacy of trees, especially forest trees, in protecting biological habitats and minimizing global warming by capturing carbon from the atmosphere. There now is a "Billion Trees" initiative, designed to raise funds for the planting of saplings in our country and others. Efforts abound to save the Redwoods, including the writings of the naturalist John Muir. In the first decade of the last century, Muir wrote, "Any fool can destroy trees. They cannot defend themselves or run away."

I live in a town, "Ridgewood" whose name connotes the importance of trees. I live off a street, "Melrose Place," which got its name from an old family apple tree orchard. Oak,

Maple, Lotus, and Pine streets interlace our towns. The ancient sentinels can still be seen around us if we look, and we still plant trees as a testament to our faith in the future. Today's sapling is both a scion of history and a future vector to the 22nd century.

*And it is not just elms we have lost. A blight nearly wiped out the Chestnut tree species during the middle of the 20th century. On the radio during the holiday season, we hear about "chestnuts roasting on an open fire." That used to be a thing: folks would gather chestnuts from a tree in their yard, and roast them and eat them. We are now left with just street names—Chestnut Street and Elm Street— and old songs and pictures as memorials to beautiful tree species that were once elemental to our landscapes.

ESSAI 28
Frost

And miles to go before I sleep.

—Robert Frost

The road trip movie is a film genre where heroes travel cross country, often across the United States, and face a succession of trials. These challenges are transformational—knowledge is acquired and persistence rewarded. On the road trip, one necessarily continues to move forward. A traveler succumbs to the momentum of travel and at times must summon commitment to continue.

Road trips can be magical in a way. We enter new and strange territory, where we do not feel totally ourselves. We venture into unfamiliar lands and have chance encounters. Intent confronts serendipity. One never knows what's next, but still moves on to find out.

In his poetry, Robert Frost captured the sense of choice and momentum we have on the road, drawing out larger life lessons. Frost finds depth in those moments of travel where we pause and confront the mystery of the future. Here is perhaps his most famous poem, "The Road Not Taken":

The Road Not Taken

Two roads diverged in a yellow wood,
And sorry I could not travel both
And be one traveler, long I stood
And looked down one as far as I could
To where it bent in the undergrowth;

Then took the other, as just as fair,
And having perhaps the better claim,
Because it was grassy and wanted wear;
Though as for that the passing there
Had worn them really about the same,

And both that morning equally lay
In leaves no step had trodden black.
Oh, I kept the first for another day!
Yet knowing how way leads on to way,
I doubted if I should ever come back.

I shall be telling this with a sigh
Somewhere ages and ages hence:
Two roads diverged in a wood, and I—
I took the one less traveled by,
And that has made all the difference.

In this poem we sense Frost himself—outside, in the woods, in autumn, leaves on the ground—facing a choice of which of two paths to take. Of the two, one seems less-trodden, grassier and therefore more desirable as perhaps the seemingly braver choice. But then, the traveler admits that the two paths are really the same, that they are equal, and, by implication, there is no real choice here at all. Still, a path is chosen, and we fast forward to the future, "ages hence." The traveler knows he will later relate the choice as somehow significant, a perhaps prideful justification that he had chosen a "road less taken" in life when in fact it was not really "less taken" at all. The choice was actually just a momentary, mental coin-toss, which has now been given significance, truly a post hoc ergo propter hoc fallacy.

Everyone who heads outside faces a choice a few steps into his or her walk. Should I turn left at the end of my street and take a well-trodden, familiar path, or should I turn right to an untested route? It is a momentarily fraught decision, but only for an instant as the subconscious, based on often little to no facts, quickly urges me one way or the other. The mind, as Frost suggests, then rationalizes the choice, even though it likely made little difference.

It is at these small junctures in life, where there are two different options forward, that we add importance to decisions that may in fact be more whim than wit. When faced with the choice of what school to attend, what job to take, or whether to have a cheeseburger or chicken sandwich, we overthink. Choices seem of such import but are only so in our heads, and in our post-rationalizations. It is not the path we choose, but perhaps the fact of continuing forward that is critical.

Frost gives us another journey of choice in "Stopping by Woods on a Snowy Evening."

Stopping by Woods on a Snowy Evening

Whose woods these are I think I know.
His house is in the village though;
He will not see me stopping here
To watch his woods fill up with snow.

My little horse must think it queer
To stop without a farmhouse near
Between the woods and frozen lake
The darkest evening of the year.

He gives his harness bells a shake
To ask if there is some mistake.
The only other sound's the sweep
Of easy wind and downy flake.

The woods are lovely, dark and deep,
But I have promises to keep,
And miles to go before I sleep,
And miles to go before I sleep.

Here we have a seeming innocuous moment. The traveler stops at night in a wood near a lake in the midst of winter. Similar to the first walk in the woods, there is nothing significant about this place. The traveler has simply noted it as a juncture where a choice is to be made, mid-journey away from landmarks. In "The Road Not Taken" the choice is between two paths, while here it is a choice first to stop and then whether to proceed. There is peacefulness and quiet to the scene. It is a spot that most people would rush through and not take notice of, especially in the cold of winter. The stopping itself is somewhat strange, as the horse notes with a shake of bells.

Life proceeds in a rush and we are often oblivious, yet there are times when we do pause and take note. We do not stop for long—just a moment to contemplate the world around us, before we think again about our commitments to others and to ourselves. Frost notes that there are promises to keep and that we all have many miles to travel before we sleep, implying so much still to do before death. Yet, it is moments like these that we treasure.

For Frost, the idea of the traveler out on the path or on the road is symbolic of the person on his or her journey of life. In our life progression we often must stop and decide on a path to take when the choices are equal. Recognizing that the choice is at hand, we need both cognizance of the immediate choice and the larger contextual awareness of life as it passes by. Frost's poems provide generous caesurae—brief moments of higher awareness that we can carry forward.

ESSAI 29
Speed

There is absolutely no reason for being rushed along with the rush.

—*Clarence Day*

Sometimes walking just feels too slow. I live in a neighborhood where I need to walk around three sides of a block to get out to the main streets and the world beyond. Making it even harder, I live at the bottom of a hill, in a shallow valley created by a stream that runs through my property. Any direction that I choose to walk necessitates going both up a hill and around. I feel trapped a bit sometimes, and the early parts of my walks just seem to go so slowly.

I've thought of different ways to speed things up so I can see more stuff when I am out and around. First, of course, there is driving. Driving is our default mode of transportation, but it is, in truth, the enemy of walking. Although driving lets one get places faster, it detracts from good observation of one's surroundings. When you are in a car, you are in a box, sealed off from the world. Even for those that have a convertible of some sort, a car is separate from nature. One must open a door, climb inside, and then close the door. In a vehicle, we are sedentary and operating machinery, no matter how rote much of our driving routes have become. We are not truly in the landscape, but gliding through it with a separateness.

My wife often cautions me to pay attention to the road because I still try to look around at the landscape when I drive. This sometimes causes the car to swerve dangerously, and it happens most often when I am driving upstate in New York or New England. Driving along, I might spot an older house— perhaps it a farmhouse, with a big barn in back. I look for a second or two to see if the barn has a stone foundation, which seems older than the barn itself, and indicates a pre-1900 origin. And then I see a large tree in the yard between the house and the barn, and I wonder when it was planted and how it withstood the test of time. All cool stuff, at least for me. But when I am in my car, the scenery whizzes by too fast, leaving my curiosity unfulfilled. Time speeds up, and the land remains out of contemplation and ken. Cars go too fast.

Biking offers another opportunity, and I often hop on my bike and pedal off as a change of pace. Because I can range further afield in the same amount of time as when I walk, a bike ride offers more opportunities to explore. Walking limits me to a two-mile radius from my home; on a bike I can head out five miles in any direction and still return home within an hour or so. For me, within a five-mile bike ride are waterfalls, large hills, stony escarpments, historic villages, 18th-century houses and inns, two rivers, three brooks, and the usual landmarks of suburban sprawl--banks, schools, supermarkets, and mini-malls. Biking is also wonderful exercise, especially in hilly areas where biking up and down hills creates its own interval training, raising your heartbeat, and then lowering it.

But biking suffers similar speed issues to cars. Biking along, one can see cool stuff, but those cool things zip by quickly. As soon as your brain recognizes a landmark as something of note and starts to give it a thought, you have ridden by it, leaving it wistfully behind with a fleeting sense of something missed. Stopping the bike would make sense, but is often awkward with your feet coming off the pedals and the bike leaning sideways as you perch awkwardly on the side of the road looking at a hill, a stream, a rock, or an old schoolhouse. In the act of cycling, there is still this disengagement with the world. The bike remains an intermediary between me and a more authentic experience. I love my bike, but, while cycling offers freedom and range, it does not lend itself to fully understanding nature and landscape.

Walking remains the best way to immerse oneself in nature without a technological intermediary. We are of nature, but we are separate from it, and bridging this separateness even partially requires us to be on foot, confronting and contemplating the land. Still, as I said, for me walking remains a bit slow at times. A good trick I've developed is to intersperse some running or jogging to move me along a bit faster and add some exercise. This is best at the start or the end of a journey. I've seen my immediate neighborhood so often that jogging out my immediate environs feels 100% okay to me. As I tire from the jog (unfortunately for me after just a quarter or a third of a mile), I switch to walking and looking around. My heart rate is up by then (which is good). The run dispersed some of my stress, and I can get into a pleasant walk and enjoy myself. If time gets short, I can do another quick run, maybe to a landmark I have in mind. There is no set approach here. I could drive to a park or a museum and then walk around. Or I can target a landmark four miles away on my bike, arrive there, and then stroll around with my notebook. Whatever works for you is what is right.

The specialness of walking, I think, comes from an awareness of a sixth sense that we have, called "proprioception." Proprioception is the feeling that we have of our physical bodies—the awareness of the placement and position of our head, torso, and limbs—as we experience the world, including our bodies' movement as we take actions.

When we walk thoughtlessly, we perceive the world as almost like a movie happening around us. Events occur, like noting a passing car or sensing the rising wind, which our brain registers and perhaps has some thoughts about—*that car is going too fast .... I left my raincoat at home.* If we walk, though, with heightened proprioception, we become more aware of ourselves and our bodies, as we exert effort and move across the ground. With an awareness of proprioception, we can break the habit of obliviousness as we build a sense of our physical selves. Once we heighten this awareness, we can truly begin to experience and enjoy what is going on around us. The feeling of one's body can increase the sensing of what is going on around us, creating a more holistic connection between the walker and his or her surroundings.

The easiest way to increase proprioception is to physically jolt ourselves by putting some stress on our bodies to stimulate awareness. This could be as simple and quick as reaching up to the sky when we exit our front door and stretching for a few seconds. Perhaps, as mentioned before, instead of starting to walk, we jog or even sprint the first 50 yards. A deep breath can often do the trick, especially if it is cold out or if the air is fragrant, as it often is in spring or fall. A second way is through some walking meditation, where we focus on our footsteps and how the steps sync with our breath until we enter into almost a walking trance, clearing the mind. And once we have a sense of ourselves, we then extend our thoughts and connect with the landscape around us.

ESSAI 30
Ridgewood

God made the country, and Man made the town.
—William Cowper

Consider Ridgewood, New Jersey: a medium-sized town; a suburb of New York City; a train stop for the New Jersey Transit railroad; a high-property-tax enclave; a village of 25,000 souls; a school district purposed for college prep; an amalgam of larger and smaller homes; an arbored and lawned landscape; a place of ridges and woods; and a land with a deep past. A history of the town written in 1900 states: "Ridgewood is remarkable for its natural beauty and the diversity of its scenery. From the ridge tops, a magnificent panorama opens to view, in some instances extending miles in all directions. At the same time, the fertile valleys between the heights and along the brooks lend an added interest to this charming locality."

Four streams of water partition Ridgewood. These streams are definitionally "brooks" in that they are smaller than rivers and creeks, generally shallow, easy to ford, and have beds of rocks over which water most often babbles. All four brooks flow in a south by southeast direction following the downward flow of the land from the Ramapo Mountains ridge northwest of town towards the Passaic River several miles south.

Up and down the east side of town is the largest brook,

named the Saddle River. I've always felt that calling the Saddle River a "river," was an exaggeration, as it is not broad, deep, or navigable. It runs alongside the Paramus Road, an original part of the pre-revolutionary Hoboken-Albany toll road that ran from the Hudson River in New Jersey up into New York State to the capital at Albany. The Saddle River was a magnet for early settlers, and older Dutch homesteads dot the nearby streets. The Saddle River source is in Rockland County in New York State, and it then tracks down through several towns before flowing through Ridgewood. In Ridgewood, the brook is part of a park with a running/walking/biking trail alongside it. South of the village, the river flows through the towns of Glen Rock, Paramus, and Saddle Brook before meeting the Passaic River, which then leads to Newark Bay. Once in Newark Bay, the water can slowly make its way through Kill Van Kull or Arthur Kill, along the shores of Staten Island, then into New York Harbor or Raritan Bay, before reaching the Atlantic Ocean.

About one mile west of the Saddle River runs the HoHoKus Brook, named after the small town north of Ridgewood. The HoHoKus Brook has a variety of sources in northwest Bergen County. Different streams merge north of town, and then the brook meanders through Ridgewood, past the town pool, the library, and the high school, before joining with the Saddle River at the southern border. The cool thing about the HoHoKus brook is its descent from the highlands northwest of town to the flatter land in town. That descent is through a gorge running below a high ridge (part of the "ridge" of Ridgewood). The gorge is visually cut off from the surrounding neighborhoods, especially when the leaves come in, and has a rough, mountain stream feel. In springtime, it is a torrent.

In the far west part of town, a small stream arises from a natural spring in a low spot where two hills come together. This brook flows through several neighborhoods, including through my own yard, and alongside an elementary school, gathering flow from other small streams, until it becomes the Diamond Brook—the main brook flowing through the towns of Glen Rock and Hawthorne on its way to the Passaic River. The natural spring, where the brook begins, hearkens to when there were many such springs, most of which are now hidden under or behind development.

Lastly, the Goffle Brook borders the southwest of Ridgewood. Goffle Brook flows down from the Ramapo ridge, through the towns of Wyckoff and Midland Park, and then down western Ridgewood. The river is dammed in Midland Park, and the original mill house from the early 19th century still stands close by. The dam and the mill are a reminder that all of the brooks mentioned here were dammed at intervals in the early 1800s to supply power to different mills.

Ridgewood was farmland in the late-17th century. The area was settled by Dutch farmers on land co-opted from a local Leni-Lenape native tribe (it is uncertain whether or how the original natives were compensated). Through the first century and a half of post-native settlement, up until the 1850s, there was no town where Ridgewood currently stands. The initial settlement of the area was antipodal, with a cluster of homes far to the east near the Saddle River and another far west along Goffle Brook. In the east, a group of farmhouses were built around the Paramus Dutch Reformed Church, which was originally built in the 1730s, was rebuilt around 1800, and is still standing today. The church is a historical landmark in this part of New Jersey: George Washington is said to have visited; and Aaron Burr married Theodosia Prevost in the church.* As regards the small community around the church, a six-lane highway, Route 17, now roars right through it, bisecting the historic cluster so that the Dutch farmhouses lie to the east of the road while the church and its graveyard are marooned on the west.

Jumping six miles to the west of the old Dutch church, where the Goffle Brook tumbles down a dam, one can see the remains of an old mill village where the Van Riper, Lydecker, and Wortendyke mills were located at various times in the first half of the 1800s. These mills were quite large and, over the course of time, ground flour and manufactured cotton fabrics. One can still see some old Dutch homes and one of the mill structures (now an antique store). The old mill pond is still there too. The area is now part of the Borough of Midland Park, but in the early 1800s, it was an industrial area. Goffle Road, paralleling the brook, ran south from this mini village to Paterson, which was a more extensive, fast-growing mill town itself in the early 19th century.

Between these two poles—the Paramus Dutch church far to the east and the Goffle mills far to the west—stretched six miles of farmland dotted with Dutch Colonial farmhouses, barns, storehouses, pens, and other accouterments of the mid-Atlantic Federal-era farming landscape. There was no town, no stores, and no schools. That all changed, though, with the coming of the railroads in the 1840s.

In 1848, the Erie Railroad constructed a spur from Paterson, New Jersey, south of present-day Ridgewood, to Suffern, New York 30 miles further north. The railroad line cut right across the farmland from south to north, equidistant from the Paramus church to the east and the Goffle mills to the west. This line initially did not have a stop in the present-day town. Later, a stop was added, and a small station, originally called Godwinsville, was built in early 1859.

The railroad station was originally designed to serve as a freight stop for the local mills, bringing in raw materials and shipping finished goods and supporting a nearby local lumber yard, but it quickly acquired an added purpose. Because the railroad connected southwards not only to Paterson but also further south to Hoboken and the ferries to Manhattan, one could board the railroad at Godwinsville and make it into lower Manhattan in a reasonable time. With the railroad and the local station, the town became commutable from New York City, and real estate development began as commercial and home plots subsumed farmland. Local land boosters decided to change the name from Godwinsville to the more pleasant sounding, "Ridgewood," reflecting the character of the land and the desire to attract new homeowners (an early development of homes was called "Ridgewood Park"). Ridgewood had plenty of available real estate as well as views from local ridges and hills of the surrounding countryside all the way to the Manhattan, and the choicest plots were taken and developed into vacation homes. What was once just farmland became a small town expanding outwards from the train station as local farms were converted into neighborhoods.

A romance made famous again 200 years later from the song "Dear Theodosia" in the musical Hamilton.

ESSAI 31
Ridgewood redux

Son take a good look around. This is your hometown.
                                    —Bruce Springsteen

In 1859, Ridgewood gained its first railroad depot: a simple rectangular wood-frame building sitting at the intersection where the town's main street, Ridgewood Avenue, crossed the north-south tracks. In 1916, the Erie Railroad decided to eliminate grade crossings to enhance safety for many small towns along its routes while simultaneously building modern stations better suited for commuter traffic. In Ridgewood, the rail tracks were raised, and Ridgewood Avenue, the main street of the town, became cut in two. Traffic from Ridgewood Avenue could no longer cross the tracks but instead was diverted a block north to an underpass. In partnership with the town, the Erie Railroad also built a new "Mission Style" commuter station complex with a landscaped town square as part of a greater beautification effort.

The early 20th century saw a proliferation of the use of Mission Style architecture in public buildings and private homes. Mission Style reflects the design of historic Spanish missions across the American southwest, leveraging stuccoed walls, Spanish-tiled roofs, and arcades. The Atchinson-Topeka-Santa Fe Railroad in the southwest United States and

California pioneered the use of the Mission Style to beautify their railroad stops. The architect-engineers of the Ridgewood station, W.W. Drinker and Frank A. Howard, drew on this trend in their design for the 1916 upgrade. The station architecture features a brick base, arcades, cream-colored stucco walls, inset decorative ceramics, and green-tiled pottery roofs connecting gable-arched end facades. Station buildings were constructed on both the east and west sides of the tracks. There were smaller sheds for the underpasses as well as awnings for the train platforms. All the elements shared the same visual dynamic, and a recent remodeling of the station in the 2010s retained the historic design.

The Ridgewood train station is the cynosure of the town. It is in the middle of the commercial district, surrounded by local shops, restaurants, and banks. The station is set amidst a landscaped parking area called Wilsey Square, which was designed and built when the Mission Style station was constructed 100 years ago. The Wilsey Square landscaping includes green grassy areas with curving walks, well-spaced trees, and stone abutments. The architecture of the train station and the surrounding landscape give a classic aesthetic to the town center. The commercial buildings surrounding the square reflect the desire for historicity, with some structures featuring Romanesque or Renaissance Revival facades, interspersed with other Tudor and Gothic style retail and office buildings. The larger commercial district beyond the square provides a catalog of styles from the original Dutch farmhouse brick to Classic Revival, Ironbound, Tudor, Art Deco, and more modern designs.

From the 1860s, home construction radiated outwards from the train station and commercial district. There is a core of homes within a mile walking distance from the train station, built mostly before 1940. Second Empire, Italianate, and Victorian homes were first constructed, extending the town environs in the late 19th century. Further out, one finds Foursquare and Craftsmen houses of the 1900s and 1910s, and then clusters of Tudors and Colonials from the 1920s to the 1950s. Amidst these are scattered Mission Style and Prairie Style examples. The more contemporary homes generally furthest out.

I live at the far end of a dead-end street about 1.1 miles from the train station. Four houses that surround mine were built in the early 1960s. As I head towards the train station and the town center, the homes get progressively older. Close to my home are 1930s Tudors, and then a 1940s colonial followed several bungalows. One then passes a series of 1910s Foursquare homes before reaching the main road where a stately Queen Anne Victorian mansion from the 1890s sits. This pattern of traveling from younger border architecture towards the older homes in the town center holds for nearly every vector to the Ridgewood town center.

There are two other dynamics to note when tracking construction eras and architecture in Ridgewood. First, the tops of ridges saw the first homes because of the desire for a cool breeze and a view, especially towards New York City. Hilltops feature the oldest and largest homes in the town. Second, amidst the radiating growth, one can still find the small Dutch farmhouses that predate the train station and the commuter suburb's growth.

Bergen County, New Jersey, where Ridgewood is located, is an older part of the country originally settled in the 1660s by Dutch heritage immigrants from New York City. Bergen County is famous for its distinctive, vernacular Dutch-style stone houses. These houses sport large red-brick construction and arching gable or gambrel wood-shingled roofs that often overhang the house-front to create an open porch. From the late 1600s until the 1840s, these stone Dutch-style houses proliferated throughout the lower Hudson Valley as the preferred style for new farmers. The local red Triassic sandstone was easily quarried and carve-able into blocks for construction. A standard template for the house was imitated throughout the area: single story, three rooms (one in front, two in back), large attic, front porch, facing southwards, often near local brooks. There was an intentional permanence to these homes signaled by the use of stone, and those stone walls and foundations have persisted through time as additions to the houses were made and facades altered.

One fun thing that I enjoy is finding those older, pre-1840 Dutch homes in Ridgewood when I go out for a walk. I look out for the local red sandstone blocks that make up the old houses' walls. The blocks often have an uneven, haphazard look due to the settling of the house over time. You can also spot the red sandstone in old garden retaining walls. I've seen vine-covered walls made of the old red stone in the back of town lots and on the borders of local parks. For some homes, the red blocks can be seen from the street just in the foundation, with a frame house built on top, suggesting the old home may have been torn down and rebuilt, or perhaps wood siding now covers the old stone walls.

A second indication of an older house is its position relative to the street. Old farmhouses are nearly always faced to the south to maximize heat capture from the sun, especially in the winter, with the kitchen located in the back on the north side where it would be cooler when cooking. The farmers also placed their homes close to the road, versus today's suburban aesthetic of having a front lawn with the house back from the street per local ordinance.

Once you know what to look for it is simple to find these Dutch homes. One walks on the older roads, usually the primary through streets. These roads predate the side streets which were later carved from the farmland as the town grew. One looks for homes that abut the road but are canted to the south and sport the red block walls or foundation. Bingo! And once you find one of these classics, it's then fun to figure out the landscape of what would have been its old farmyard. Are there the remnants of a well? Where would the barn have been (or has it been repurposed as a garage)? Where is the nearby stream? Is this house near a historic mill? What alterations have been made to the home? Each of these homes has a small tale to tell—a bit of visual history to be detected, pondered, and enjoyed.

ESSAI 32
Marching

For we cannot tarry here,
We must march my darlings, we must bear the
brunt of danger,
We the youthful sinewy races, all the rest on
us depend.

—Walt Whitman

Histories of the Civil War give short shrift to the distances that the eastern-theater soldiers of the Union and Confederate armies had to march. I've driven from southern Pennsylvania, down the Shenandoah Valley to central Virginia, and it is a long trip--165 miles through rough terrain of mountains and valleys, woods, and fields. In the history books, we hear of the different armies with their generals moving across the countryside almost like chess pieces, shifting magically here and there through central Virginia and the Shenandoah Valley, or up into Maryland and Pennsylvania, or down towards Richmond and eventually Appomattox.

General Robert E. Lee's Confederate "Army of Northern Virginia" became famous for the speed with which it marched. It was able to gain tactical advantage despite having fewer soldiers than their Union foe. However, when Lee's army first traveled to Maryland in 1862, marching from the outskirts of Washington, D.C. up to and then over the Potomac River, Lee lost an estimated 17,000 men to straggling, with his army shrinking from 57,000 soldiers to 40,000 immediately before the battle of Antietam. The Confederate military lacked shoes and often marched and fought barefoot.

On a long march, soldiers straggle and fall out of line because they search for water, stop to eat or to find food, or simply because they are tired and decide to nap near the roadside. There were few disciplined marches on either side during the Civil War. Regimental formations that started in line on the road in the morning fell apart into haphazard groups and individual walkers by midday. Armies on the march staggered and stopped and started along the roads and spread out into surrounding farmlands and woods.

The experience of the march could be horrific. One soldier wrote, "the sun was like a furnace, the dust thick and suffocating." Another soldier at the end of a long day describes the men as, "tired, sore, sleepy, and hungry, dusty and dirty as pigs." Some historical novels have put into words the experience of the march. In *Killer Angels*, the great story of the Gettysburg campaign based on historical soldier narratives, Michael Shaara writes of the Union Army's journey up to Pennsylvania:

> *...you could sleep on your feet on the long marches. You set your feet to going and after a while they went by themselves and you sort of turned your attention away and your feet went on walking painlessly, almost without feeling, and gradually you closed down your eyes so that all you could see were the heels of the man in front of you, one heel, other heel, one heel, other heel, and so you moved dreamily in the heat and dust....*

Indeed, war was a long journey. Even in defeat, fighting for the wrong cause, the Confederate soldiers were described this way: "On they come, with the old swinging route step and swaying battle flags. In the van, the proud Confederate ensign. Before us in proud humiliation stood ... men whom neither toils and sufferings, nor the fact of death could bend from their resolve."

In the armies, there was heavy marching and light marching. Heavy marching involved moving the entire camp to a new location; soldiers carried large packs with clothing, food, equipment, and keepsakes. Lighter marching occurred more en route to an actual battle with only a smaller knapsack; men could move faster and more flexibly, ready to fight. I have never done any marching, and I find the prospect of either the heavy march with a 50-pound pack or a light march with battle imminent intimidating, to say the least. I find it strange that my heart falters today at easy tasks when armies of 100,000 seemed ready and able to march onward.

Much of the country in the 1860s was open farmland with long sight lines, dotted with barns, farmhouses, and fences. Today, trees have repopulated the landscape. I still try to imagine what it must have been like on those marches. When I walk past an open area or get to a spot on a hill where I can see more of a vista, I sometimes squint my eyes a bit and imagine it is 1862 or 1863.

I have an image in my mind of how to march, how to chew up the miles with my feet, how to journey afar, and how to embark on a quest. I'm not referring to our light strolls through suburban neighborhoods, or sojourns in parks, or a stroll on a city sidewalk, or an hour hike through some tamed state forest, or one of those power walks with an electronic wrist band that counts our steps. The image I have in my mind is Liam Neeson, playing the role of the 18th century Scottish hero Rob Roy in the eponymous film. In the movie, there is a lot of trekking going on. Rob Roy walks with a purpose—chasing down cattle thieves to bring them to justice, heading back home to reunite with wife and kin, journeying to town to cut a financial deal with the local lord, running off to the hills to hide out and play a bit of Robin Hood, and finally heading to a duel to redeem his and his wife's honor.

Rob Roy and his clansmen all walk leaning forward like a dog on a scent, tackling the hills and heath of the Scottish Highlands, striding in their tartan kilts and boots, oblivious to the typically cloudy rainy weather. The Scots look rough, with long disheveled hair, shadows of beard, flushed faces, tall and lean, muscular calves thumping along under the kilts. These men are armed with weapons and capable of mayhem, but also kind, humorous, loyal, and faithful.

The Scottish Whiskey brand, Johnny Walker, captures this striding/walking Scottish ethic in their "Just Keep Walking" ad campaign where they co-opt the determined Highlands walker image as aspirational. The Scots of the 18th century were downtrodden but had a devotion to family and tribe and a dream of betterment that willed their legs to keep moving forward, despite persecution. This deep-rooted willfulness feels strange and so different from our contemporary motives, beyond our ken but still captivating and aspirational.

So much of human history is on foot. Marches, pilgrimages, invasions, and evacuations all require will and sacrifice for accomplishment. In Arabic, the word "hajj" means to intend a journey. For a Muslim, the Hajj is the great pilgrimage that they take once in their lifetime to Mecca to honor Allah, a physical homage to their religious tradition. The Hajj journey culminates in a series of rituals in Mecca, including the Tawaf, where one walks seven times around the holy cube of the Kaaba, followed by the Sa'ay, running or walking seven times between the hills of Safa and Marwah.

The idea of mass pilgrimage to a holy place is perhaps the

ultimate act of walking. Pilgrims forsake the mundane and give themselves up to the journey as a culmination of their spirituality. The mission is sacredness made manifest—a physical, laborious act that is a testament to devotion, in much the same way that the will of an army is a testament to its patriotism.

In the Middle Ages, masses of Christian pilgrims from Europe journeyed to Jerusalem to worship at sites made holy by Jesus. What they sought was meaning--it was less about the destination and more about the journey itself, the deprivation and the travail, the yearning and the dedication, the camaraderie and communion. So important did these Christian expeditions become that wars were fought—the Crusades of the late Middle Ages—to confront the Muslim takeover of Jerusalem due to the fear that the Holy Land would be closed off to future pilgrims.

In the United States, the great pilgrimages of our history have vectored west and have sought to conquer the geographic barriers of rivers, deserts, and mountains. Early pioneers in the late 18th Century had to overcome the forests and mountains of the Appalachians to reach the Ohio and Mississippi. Later, pioneers in the 1840s crossed the prairie's vast grasslands and conquered the Rockies en route to Oregon and Northern California. We have numerous stories of Native Americans forced from their lands and made to walk incredible distances to be resettled. The "Trail of Tears," taken by the Cherokees of Georgia and Alabama across the south to Oklahoma was aptly named.

The great marches in our modern times are now imbued with social meaning. Gandhi's non-violent Salt March in India in 1930 was a protest against British rule, taxation, and suppression. Gandhi inspired the march led by Martin Luther King from Selma to Montgomery, Alabama in 1964. That march was a physical act by real people, imbued with an explicit religious spirit that confronted authorities. It was both a reflection and a continuation in a way of the redemptive marching of the Union Army in the Civil War. It was a pivotal moment, and the drama of it forced recognition of the need for outside change to reform southern laws.

For me, the heroism of the past raises a challenge about accomplishment today. Though we are not pilgrims, protestors, soldiers, or revolutionaries, perhaps we should be. Even as a metaphor, the idea of striding with a specific purpose can serve us powerfully as a necessary goad. Life is too easy, too sedate. We need the reification of our mission through the physical act. Life is a journey, but only if it is not clichéd, and if intention, commitment, and action are real.

ESSAI 33
Suburbs

Through the suburbs sleepless people stagger, as though just delivered from a shipwreck of blood.
—Frederico Garcia Lorca

Allow me a bit of a rant.

Why is it that in TV sitcoms we so often see a depiction of suburban family life where one character, usually one of the two parents, appears stressed out, highly emotional, and sometimes in a rage, while another parent comes across as a clueless imbecile, saying stupid things, misapprehending what is going on? In some episodes, the stressed parent is the butt of the joke; in others, it is the moronic one that drives the laughs—a tag team of depicted dysfunction.

Why is it a trope of suburbs in movies that there is a murderous evil lurking behind the happy facade of everyday life and that this evil most often attacks children and teens? Drama gets painted on the boring suburban template: a non-conforming stranger comes to stir things up; a sensitive artiste violates the social norms; or, maybe just something weird happens in that old abandoned house down at the corner.

Our perception of the suburbs is that they have a bland, conservative sameness—house after house, lawn after lawn, street after street—an architecture of monotony. Cool they are not. Suburbs have a role in our culture as the normalcy counterpoint to both city and country. City life is inherently exciting, creative, young, intellectual, sexual, and subversive. City dwellers live amidst the action, whether that is the business dynamism of high finance, advertising, and technology, or the milieu of art, music, and literature, or the nightlife of bars, restaurants, and clubs. Against all of these dimensions, the suburbs comparatively fall short.

Similarly, suburbs contrast poorly with the country. Out in the countryside, nature is more real, less orchestrated, less linear, and less demanding. Pastoral farmland and cottaged seashores are escapes where routines relax, and fresh air imbues and renews. We touch nature out in the country with both an immediacy and a sense of the underlying history. Country life is more in touch with the past, and therefore better than modern life, especially the implied modernity of everyday suburbia.

The 1933 *Oxford English Dictionary* defines a suburb as: "the country lying immediately outside a town or city; more particularly, those residential parts belonging to a town or city that lie immediately outside or adjacent to its walls or boundaries." A suburb is defined by something it is not; it is not of the city but is defined by its proximity to the city. The word came from the latin "suburbium" which itself came from the Latin roots of "sub" (under), and "urbs" (city) to designate a separate, often outlying section. The word came to English from Old French, which itself came from medieval Latin. It first came to use in England in the late 14th and early 15th centuries as cities expanded in Tudor times. The derivation and early use of the word suggest something inferior, something less than the city. If the original Roman idea had been to designate these outside-city developments as a good thing, as perhaps coequal, they could have created a word like "propurbs", combining "prope" (near or alongside) with "urbs" (city). But they did not.

The suburbs were "sub" or under the city, lesser than the city. In both Rome and Tudor England, suburbs were often slums for those who could not afford to live in the city, an annoyance to travelers who had to journey through them.

Our perception of suburbs in the United States is defined by the growth of the car-suburbs during the post-World War II baby boom. Lakewood, California near Los Angeles and Levittown, New York outside New York City on Long Island were the prototypical post-war suburbs. They were noted for uniform sized lots, limited choice for house layouts (Levittown was almost all Cape Cod design), regulated setbacks and front lawns, a shift from the front porch to the backyard patio for socializing, and unfortunately, racial segregation policies.

These neighborhoods created a cookie-cutter consistency that informs our perceptions today. The twin desire of low-cost home ownership (financed by tax deductions for owners and loan guarantees for banks by the federal government) and white flight escape from diversifying cities led to the proliferation of suburbs we see today. I remember the "I Love Lucy" story arc, where the Ricardo family lived in New York City (early 1950s), but by the end of the decade had an ideal home in the suburb of Westport, Connecticut.

The Lakewood/Levittown suburban development model persisted for over 50 years, through the mid-2000s, where we saw a proliferation of new building (the "McMansions") financed by the explosion in available mortgage financing during the housing bubble. The burst of the bubble in 2008, in a way, was a bursting of the overall suburban expectation. The ideal of homeownership became a nightmare of debt, and many of the McMansions were abandoned, with yards overgrown and flat-screen televisions dismantled.

Today, we are seeing a revolt against the suburbs with the recreation of pedestrian city life in multi-use developments, where condominiums or townhouses are built within walking distance of retail and restaurants. We also see a return to city living, as new housing developments emerge amidst or near the old city downtowns. Part of this is a rejection of the inefficiency of homeownership—the cost of debt, the caring for the home and the yard, and the negative environmental consequences. We can now call for cars to come to us, have merchandise and food delivered, and work from home too. The traditional stand-alone home just seems to make less sense.

I don't think, though, that we should throw the suburban baby out with the bathwater. Suburban life can still be a good thing. Our suburbs have lost much of their original intent, but there is a path forward for us to a positive sensibility that better reflects the initial suburban impulse. How can we recapture ideas that were present when suburbs first formed way back in the 19th century, but that we have lost today? For those of us doomed to continue to live in these enclaves of ennui, I believe there is a way forward, delving deeper into the whatnot of our whereabouts.

(continued in next essai)

ESSAI 34
Homo Suburbus

History is the witness that testifies to the passing of time; it illuminates reality, vitalizes memory, provides guidance in daily life, and brings us tidings of antiquity.

—*Marcus Tullius Cicero*

As mentioned in previous essais, I reside in Ridgewood, New Jersey, a New York suburb about 17 miles from Manhattan. I've now lived here for 19 years, longer than I've lived in any other place. For worse or better, I am now of "New Jersey," evolved into "Homo Suburbus" with the accouterments of house, lawn, dog, patio, and a roof that really needs fixing. A few years ago, I decided to explore this town where I live. I wanted to learn its landscape and its history, but beyond that, I wanted to understand some of the original impulses behind town creation. I started by trying to understand the initial impetus--the growth of railroad transportation in the mid-19th century--then segued into an exploration of the cultural/aesthetic impulse underlying early suburbs. In the end, I took a look at the historical development of my specific neighborhood.

I am fascinated by the growth of the railroad suburbs in the northeast. I've lived in Boston, Chicago, Philadelphia, and New York, as well as Long Island and now in northern

New Jersey. When I was young, my father commuted from our home in Huntington (on Long Island) into Manhattan each day on the Long Island Railroad. He would take the train from Huntington to Woodside Avenue in Queens and then transfer to the New York IRT (Interborough Rapid Transit) subway train, now the "7" train, to head into Grand Central Station in Manhattan. It was then just a short walk of a few blocks to his office at 90 Park Avenue South. When we moved to Chicago, Dad commuted on the C&NW (Chicago & Northwestern Railroad) from the northern suburb of Glencoe, where we lived then. I took the same railroad, but for just a few stops, from Glencoe to Winnetka, where I attended high school. When I lived in New York City, I took the Long Island Railroad myself, but outwards on summer weekends to various beach rental houses with friends.

I now live in a commuter suburb in New Jersey, whose activity in the morning and evening revolves around the departures and arrivals of the train. I never had a job where I took a daily train to the city, so the commuter trains always retained for me an element of novelty and romance. When I take a train into the city, the act of buying the tickets, waiting on the platform, selecting a seat, getting my ticket punched, peering through the window, and anticipating the final stop, all still feel special—so different than the usual car rides we take.

When the commuter trains first were built, they did create a bit of magic for folks. For those who lived in the city, the railroad represented an escape to the country, a weekend home, a country villa, or bungalow away from the crowding, the smell, and the noise. Trains evolved in the late Victorian era from a focus on freight and long-distance travel to shorter journeys, into and out of cities, faster and with more scheduled trains. It became possible at the turn of the 20th century not just to escape out to the country periodically, but to live in the country daily and commute in.

Suburban development in the United States began in the 1840s. It was driven by a desire of wealthier city dwellers to get out of the city on weekends, and enabled by the expansion of train service outwards from the city. The horticulturalist and landscape designer Andrew Jackson Downing gave voice and definition in the 1840s to the ideals of exurban village and home life, promoting cottages and villas landscaped for delight and social intercourse. In 1848 he advocated for "lawns, fine trees, shady walks, and beautiful shrubs and flowers" to promote "health and spirits, of exercise in the pure open air, amid the groups of fresh foliage ... with a chat with friends and pleasures shared with them." This sentiment became a driving force for the wealthy to seek weekend homes or to move entirely out of city centers. Throughout the Northeast and Midwest, railroads and local stations radiated outwards from the older urban areas. Villages near the cities began to expand and gentrify from prior rural roots.

If at first the suburban impulse had an idyllic tinge—the desire for country villas, fresh air, and escape from city life—new suburban towns quickly evolved more prosaically as real estate ventures. Developers bought up local farms, combined them into large parcels, and then mapped out streets with house plots. Intentional town design replaced haphazard home building. Early examples of this dynamic are Llewellyn Park 12 miles from New York in New Jersey, Shaker Heights outside Cleveland, and Forest Hills in Queens, New York.

In 1868, Frederick Law Olmsted and his partner Calvert Vaux, the designers of Central Park in New York City, were commissioned to create a design for a new "Suburban Village" called "Riverside" at a freight stop on the Burlington train line nine miles from downtown Chicago on the Des Plaines River.

In his Riverside proposal Olmsted wrote of city life: "proximity of dwellings which characterizes all strictly urban neighborhoods, is a prolific source of morbid conditions of the body and mind, manifesting themselves chiefly in nervous feebleness or irritability and various functional derangements."

Riverside was to be a counterpoint to the congestion of the city. The Olmsted-Vaux design forsook the traditional checkerboard street matrix, opting instead for curving streets and spaces for public parks, all within walking distance of the train. The roads were to have "gracefully-curved lines, generous spaces, and the absence of sharp corners, the idea being to suggest and imply leisure, contemplativeness, and happy tranquility." Turf and trees would abound. The houses would be set apart, yet local gathering areas would be within walking distance. The Olmsted-Vaux vision sought to combine the need for nature without the isolation of the countryside. Nature would become a simultaneously vivifying and relaxing element in the community, as the new home-owners strolled amidst the curving streets with hills, trees, and grass. Their plan became a template for other suburban communities, where roads and lots were pre-planned by developers and in advance to avoid scatter-shot home and street design.

I live in a neighborhood in Ridgewood, New Jersey that captures elements of the Olmsted-Vaux vision. My surrounding streets were laid out at the turn of the 20th century on land carved from four previous Dutch-heritage farms (owned then by Ackerman, Ackerman, Marinus, and Quackenbosh). Unlike neighborhoods closer to the center of town, the streets of my neighborhood were designed with curves at intersections instead of corners. These curves create small, triangular parks at street junctures beautifying the community and easing driving. The first houses built were large Queen Ann Victorians, nearer to the main through-road, and over 30 years the neighborhood filled in. Many of the second wave of homes, 1900-1910, are classic Foursquare, close to the street with shared driveways and large front porches. The houses get progressively younger as one moves from the main road further south into the neighborhood, with some Craftsman-style homes and Dutch Colonials, followed by Mission Style, Tudors, Colonial Revival, and even some interspersed Ranches and Cape Cods from the 1950s and 60s.

I reviewed the historical town maps in our local library and traced my neighborhood's progression from farmland to complete community. An 1861 map shows mostly farms, with no town where Ridgewood would eventually be--just the recently built Erie Railroad Station. Both the 1861 and 1867 maps note the names of the families who own the different farms; one of them, the Quackenbosh farmhouse, still exists today (I walk my dog by it a couple of times a week). The 1876 and 1896 maps show the growth of the town streets near the railroad station, but little action where my neighborhood now is—just a stub of one of the avenues that would later expand out. The 1912 map, though, was quite different. It showed all the avenues and streets of my neighborhood laid out, along with the individual lots. Few of the eventual homes were actually built at the time, just some of the aforementioned Victorians, Foursquares, and a couple of Craftsmen. Strangely, the 1912 map included several streets that do not exist today, including a "Marlborough Avenue," as the map represented the developers' future plan and not the actual streets at that time. The 1926 map showed more cross streets, but then those disappear in the 1938 map. Street names seemed to change map to map as well: a Vista Street becomes Melrose Place; a Hillcrest Street becomes Grant Avenue. Fast forward to 1965 and the geography finally becomes fully recognizable. All the streets are now shown with their correct name, including my own, which was developed around 1961.

The French social critic and filmmaker Guy Debord defined the term "psychogeography" as "the study of the precise laws and specific effects of the geographical environment, consciously organized or not, on individuals' emotions and behavior." We all have a psychogeography—a way of thinking and feeling about and identifying with our locales. Discovering the origins of our neighborhoods and our towns can inform our psychogeographic sensibility about suburban life. There is historical depth to our seemingly ordinary communities. By delving into the raison d'etre of our environs, we can bring curiosity to the commonplace. A deeper knowledge of our neighborhoods can lead to more satisfaction with our circumstances. The study of our street layouts, the local architecture, and the origins of our towns and villages are the means to a conceptual organization of our local space. There is a psychological and intellectual satisfaction to be had.

ESSAI 35
Place

*To this place, and the kindness of these people,
I owe everything. Here I have lived a quarter
of a century, and have passed from a young to
an old man.*

*—Abraham Lincoln
(Farewell address in Springfield, 1861)*

It is funny where we end up. My street address is "10 Carolina Place," and I have lived here for 15 years with my wife and three children. The street name is ironic and somewhat humorous for those who know me. I attended college at the University of Virginia, whose rival is the University of North Carolina. How the heck did I end up on a street whose name pays homage to the enemy? In fact, how the heck did the road get the name Carolina in the first place? Charlotte, North Carolina is 652 miles away, and there is nothing about the street that is like living in North Carolina and even less like South Carolina. Carolina Place is just a small piece of pavement in the chilly northeast where some of us sport accents more Soprano-like than genteel. We have Maple and Beech trees, not Live Oak or Palmetto. I should just be thankful I did not end up on a "Syracuse Avenue" or god forbid "Duke Boulevard."

I do not live on a street or road, but on a "place": Carolina

Place. I have placed myself in a place on a place and have remained in that place for quite a long time. The street name "place" derives from the Latin, "platea," meaning street area or courtyard. A more expansive meaning of place can be found in the French "Place," as in the Place de la Concorde or the Place de la Bastille, examples of the large plazas one sees in Paris. The other sense of "place," though, is in the naming of a manor house or home. We find this in the Cornish word "plas" which means mansion or manor house. Here in the United States "place" has come to mean a short street or a cul-de-sac ("cul-de-sac" is French for "bottom of a sack"). It is indeed a short street I live on, as there are only two houses, mine and my neighbors, both of us abutting a dead end. Carolina Place is certainly not a large plaza, nor is my house a mansion.

My place is humble, and the street is placid, but I guess there is some drama in the fact that I live on a "dead end"? Dead end is a curious phrase. The meaning is straightforward and effective in reference to streets. The descriptor conveys the finality and lack of options at the end of a road. Dead ends have amputated futility. "Warning!" the dead-end sign implies, "if you proceed down this street, you will reach an end after which you will find no further life--no people, houses, lawns, or cars! This street dies out, and your progress will be halted!"

A more expansive meaning of "dead end" has emerged over time, especially in reference to careers—"dead-end job"—capturing this same effective sense of finality. There is no way out from death; there is no further life, and choices are gone when we reach our personal dead ends. Indeed the first reference to dead-end streets comes from Leon Battista Alberti, where he calls them out as a ploy in town design that could confuse enemy invaders. If a group of soldiers turned down a street that dead ended, they could be trapped there and slain.

When I was in grade school, I lived on Rope Court, which

was just a big paved circle surrounded by five houses. Our life there was happily circumscribed. We played with kids from the other homes, and we played out in the court itself, setting up bases and playing kickball in the evening. Courts are also technically dead-end streets, but not really. There is no end to a circle: a car enters and then curves by the houses progressing to exit whence it came. The circle itself creates the feel of a plaza, with all of the houses facing inward providing a bit of drama and action like the quadrangle of a college or the courtyard of a hotel. A court has a heightened sense of formality à la law courts or the court or retinue of a king or queen. The words "place" and the "court" devolved from something grander in the old world to something more commonplace in the new. Real estate developers are not stupid, as who wouldn't rather live in the rarified environs of a "court" as opposed to the plebeian "street."

Speaking of plebeian, there are also a bunch of "lanes" in my neighborhood, and, after living on Rope Court, my family moved to Grouse Lane when I was 9. Lanes have humility. They turn up in nursery rhymes, like "Baa Baa Black Sheep" where some of the wool may go to "the little boy who lives down the lane," or remember the "Muffin Man, that lives in Drury Lane?" Lanes are small streets that have a sense of being hemmed in by hedges or perhaps stone walls; or in cities, a lane is like an alley cutting between two buildings. Choosing a lane hints at making a choice and sticking to it, or perhaps not being able to divert from it. Runners must stay in their lanes on running tracks. We may perhaps choose life in the fast lane.

From Grouse Lane, my family moved to Crescent Drive (and later to Old Harbor Drive), where I lived when I earned my driver's license and began driving. When I think of "drives" I think of curving roads through parks or park-like areas, and Crescent Drive does curve left through a park before arcing rightwards through my old neighborhood. New York's Central Park has the curving and swooping East and West Drives, although cars are now banned from Central Park entirely. I wonder if they will rename the Drives as "The West Walk"? "The East Bike"? Hopefully, we have moved beyond "The North Rollerblade!"

At the University of Virginia, I lived in the McCormick Road dorms. Roads connote something more important than lanes or courts in that they connect one to some significant destination. I think that is because the common usage of roads is as a thoroughfare between cities, out in the country, cutting across the landscape. Jack Kerouac's novel *On the Road*, speaks to his cross country epic and not any urban meanderings. Willie Nelson's song, "On the Road Again," speaks to the desire to get back to the road with friends—"like a band of gypsies we go down the highway." Once we escape from city streets and avenues or emerge from our village ways and places, we can get on the road and experience the freedom and romance of heading through unknown lands, discovering something new. The road also has dangerous mythology for us, as in Cormac McCarthy's post-apocalyptic novel, *The Road*, where a father and son seek salvation traveling across a hellish landscape. I hope to never be on the "road to perdition," but to simply cruise on the road of life. The novelist Patrick Rothfuss writes, "A long stretch of road will teach you more about yourself than a hundred years of quiet introspection."

In my 20s, I lived in New York City, amidst the grid of east to west streets and north to south avenues. The word "street" came about because of the need to describe a paved route larger than a path or alley or lane. Streets feel less rural, very much of the city or the town like 34th street or Main Street. Streets can have their own infamies such as Bourbon Street, Beale Street, or Lombard Street.

Avenues indicate something more imposing and monumental than streets. They signal less a connecting road, but more an approach to something grand. A few hundred years ago, one would ride a carriage up an estate "avenue" to the front of a palace or mansion, and avenues today retain this feel of nobility. The word itself has the suggestion of heading towards a venue, which makes one think of sporting events or concerts. The Avenue des Champs-Elysees in Paris runs from the Place de la Concorde up to the Arc de Triomphe. Fifth Avenue in midtown New York runs from Grand Army Plaza, at the southeast corner of Central Park, down to Washington Square Park with its own copy of the Arc de Triomphe. Michigan Avenue in Chicago and Pennsylvania Avenue in Washington, D.C. share a similar monumentality.

In my time in New York City, I lived on 85th street and later on 71st street, before moving to a high-rise on 3rd avenue for a few final years. I've lived on other lanes, streets, and roads since then, too, before ending up where I am now. The places where we live provide markers in our personal history, mapping memories, and providing context. We are encouraged to find our happy place, but I think our happy place is not dependent on location but rather what we bring to the places where we live. Carolina Place would be just another street unless imbued with intent and story.

ESSAI 36
Observations

Deign on the passing world to turn thine eyes,
And pause a while from learning to be wise.

—Samuel Johnson

Outdoor spaces are created with intent. Landscape forms and structures are not just pretty to look at, not just wallpaper as we pass by, but possess deeper meaning. Observation is the essential task of our minds. We must use our brains as we experience the outdoors, adopt a sense of curiosity and perhaps wonder at the world around us. Curiosity about the structured landscape stimulates the inquisitive, detecting, problem-solving mind. This is our brain put to its best purpose, one of openness and discovery, which broadens spirit. Whether we are examining the functionality of architecture or the aesthetics of natural phenomena, our minds think and then our souls are triggered, whether we feel it in that instant or not. I find enlightenment contemplating the 200-year-old tree, the Art Deco post office building, the escarpment rising above a cloven stream, the cobbled downtown street, the geologic strata in a railroad cut, a mansard-roofed villa, the rolling meadow of a local park, and an old map from the town library.

From a perch about five or so feet above the ground, atop a swivel hinge that allows 270 degrees of movement up and down and side to side, backed by a high-performance computer unmatched for its interpretive capability, our primary sensory organs rest on one of the best observational platforms in the animal kingdom. Just look around a bit, and take in both the scope of what you can see and the detail with which you can see it. Standing on my front lawn with my dog, Josie, nearby, I can look upwards at the blue sky or downwards at the garden. Josie experiences a narrower world from just 20 inches off the ground and mostly looks downwards, relying less on her eyes and more on her nose. Humans can gaze up to the stars in the firmament, down to our firmly planted feet, or straight out to a distant horizon. Perhaps we love vacationing at the beach so much because of these precise sight lines—the white sand of the beach in our toes, the rippling ocean breakers twinkling in the sunshine, the broad horizon randomly dotted with distant ships, and perhaps the fiery glow of a setting sun.

French Impressionists captured best the variegated vision one has outdoors—the shading and dappling of browns, greens, and blues. Monet's waterlilies, Pissarro's country-scapes, and Manet's greenswards all portray a reality of color as perceived by the eye but not yet interpreted by the brain. The browns and beiges of people or structures are treated coequally with the verdure of surrounding nature. Nature's greenery resonates, as what we usually experience as background becomes foreground.

So it is with what we see ourselves. The human eye can detect minute variances in shades of green, an evolutionary adaptation to distinguish the vast variety of plants in nature and to perceive lurking danger. There are shades of emerald, jade, olive, and lime. The green around us can be verdant, leafy, or grassy. For sustenance, we must eat our greens. To be ecologically aware is to be labeled "green." Green is the first color--the color of fruit before it is ripe, the color of immaturity. The army recruit was "green"—untrained, unpolished, untested, and ingenuous.

Chlorophyll is the green pigment in plants, and the way it works is that the plant needs to absorb non-green colors in the spectrum like red and blue for the chemical reaction of photosynthesis while reflecting out the green light which is not required. Green is thus the unneeded hue in chemical nature, the color that is rejected and spewed out. It sits in the middle of the light spectrum, halfway between blue and yellow, where we can see its subtle variations.

Green is a rejection of light, but is the indicator of life. It is often forgotten in its ubiquity, but craved in its absence. The denuded city-scape is ameliorated by lining streets with trees. The anticipation of spring is heightened by the first peek of a perennial stalk. Our gaze swivels back and forth, peering for new growth, symbolizing the emergence of life itself.

So what is the best way to start observing? The phenomenologist philosophers in the 1920s talked of observing "phenomena," and they described a specific, intentional way to see and study objects. What was important for them was not understanding context or history, or cause and effect, but the act of observation itself. The philosopher Edmund Husserl who defined and initiated the phenomenology approach, wrote, "Natural objects ... must be experienced before any theorizing about them can occur." Phenomenology asks us to start by simply observing the factual presence of the things in front of us:

> *The sidewalk on which I am walking consists of concrete sections. Those sections have shifted and are uneven, as I see the push of tree roots which have grown beneath. There are cracks in the sidewalk, and grass is growing in those cracks. Each sidewalk section requires one and a quarter steps to pass over it.*

We first observe--renouncing thinking, classifying, or projecting--and in observing, we achieve a heightened presence. As Husserl writes, the goal is true experience, "intuiting that grasp of the object in the original."

When we drive to our workplace or schools each day, we sometimes arrive without consciousness of the drive itself, not remembering the roads, the buildings, and the stoplights that we just journeyed by. Perhaps we were buried in a reverie of worry or planning. The result is that we missed a small part of our life, or better said, we inadvertently spent a small piece of our lives amidst our thoughts instead of in real time in the real world. Phenomenology seeks to address this. It is demanding. It is never passive but requires a mindset that is different from our usual judging, evaluating mind. This type of thinking can be a jumping-off point awakening us to the present moment and bringing a more genuine sense of self, grounded in truth, with our minds exercised in necessary simplicity.

So much of what we see outside is familiar, especially the immediate environs of our own homes and neighborhoods. There is nothing new. Nothing has changed. The house across the street is still that same gray with those hedges that need trimming. The tree at the corner has been there forever. We need a wake-up call—a mental jolt that inspires us to peer around and seek difference and novelty.

We do not want to simply be part of the world's fabric, seamless and inert; we are not just a static piece of a mosaic. Although we are elementally of our ecosystems, we can seek to stand out by leveraging our intentional awareness and our latent ability to disrupt. We can aspire to be the seam in the fabric or the piece of the puzzle that doesn't quite fit.

The French existentialist philosopher, Maurice Merleau-Ponty spoke of this idea, labeling it a "chiasm." This word comes from the Greek letter X (chi), and it connotes the concept of the linking of two things, almost but not entirely in mirror image. The phrase: "I am natural, but I am separate from nature" is a chiasm. I am made of the same elements as all things natural in the world, but I have the unique ability to stand apart and study those elements. I am a seamless part of the natural world, but I can observe and change the natural world. I encounter the world, and the world encounters me. I change the world and the world changes me.

When we are out and around, we can extend our senses and connect with the landscape around us, while remaining separate and studying it. We are ambiguous when we walk, and awareness of this ambiguity is what makes our strolls essential. We neither want to isolate from the world nor want to lose ourselves in it fully either. We want the feel of harmony with our outdoor environment, but we also desire strangeness too. And it is this dialectic from sensory observation to connection, understanding, and analysis, and then on to the next consideration which is what life is and what our journeys can make us aware of. In the process, we become amazed and astonished as the mosaic breaks up and then reestablishes itself. Capturing this astonishment takes what seems ordinary and makes it rediscovered, reframed, and transformed.

ESSAI 37
More Observations

No matter where you live, you will find that your city, county, town, or neighborhood has characteristics common to cities, counties, towns, and neighborhoods nearly everywhere. In his classic handbook on environmental design, *A Pattern Language*, Christopher Alexander posits this commonality, stating that there is a language for the built environment which is the sum of 253 "Patterns" that exist and persist in constructed landscape and architecture.

According to Alexander, "Each Pattern describes a problem, which occurs over and over again in our environment, and then describes the core of the solution to the problem." For example, Alexander's Pattern #49 is titled "Looped Local Roads," which begins with a problem (cars will speed on straight roads cutting through residential neighborhoods) and provides a solution (roads in residential areas should curve and loop around to discourage fast cut-throughs).

Patterns are interlinked and include broad concepts like "agricultural valleys" and "communities of 7000," smaller patterns like "ring roads" and "accessible greens," and quotidian solutions like "bus stop" and "half-hidden garden." Alexander believes the patterns are archetypal, deeply embedded in what humans have needed physically, socially, and aesthetically through time. Importantly, design elements interlink: a "neighborhood" pattern needs component patterns of "green space" and "stands of trees" without which there is a sense of something missing.

Informed by Alexander's "Pattern" theory, we can begin to notice, and perhaps even note some of the patterns we see and how they come together. This is more than the individual intent and choices of the architects and builders; it is about delving into the superego of the landscape, the repetition of ideas in place and time. Alexander equates these patterns in landscape design to language, positing a poetry of human habitation and experience.

Sometimes our days are so busy that no time remains for ourselves. Our only free moments are early in the morning or later in the evening. In the spring and summer, morning and evening often offer the best light of the day. It is no accident that film directors choose the red and gold saturated light of pre-sunset and post-dawn for many outdoor shots. The fall and winter months, though, are a different story, as the edges of the day are relegated to times of darkness.

There is a hesitancy to heading out into the dark. Our genes have encoded a fear of night into our psyches. Other animals are more adapted to the darkness. In my early morning, pre-light sojourns in Connecticut years ago, I often came across scurrying critters—moles, groundhogs, raccoons, foxes, and deer—running across streets or scampering along hedges, out scavenging for food. Sensing their presence and seeing their wide glowing eyes turning my way always startled me and gave me a short adrenaline rush. I was never really in danger, but the night's uncertainty and surprises left me wary and on edge.

Luckily it is never really that dark in most of the places we live. Refulgent starlight and moonlight illuminate cloudless nights, often quite brightly. On cloudy evenings, the sheen of towns and cities reflect off the sky with a yellowish glow. For me, away to the southeast each night, the orange glow of New York City fills half the sky, drowning out starlight. Although street lights can offer solace, they sometimes appear forlorn as a glowing sentinel trying to stave off the gloom. Other lights peek out from house windows, porches, and garages. In town, there are stoplights and glowing signs in shop windows. Snow makes the light even brighter, gathering and reflecting it more strongly to our eyes. We all understand what Clement Clarke Moore meant when we wrote, "the moon on the breast of the new fallen snow gave the lustre of midday to objects below." The night is not so much dark, as it is just different.

And it is that difference which we want to experience. The landscape historian John Stilgoe uses the word "benighted" to describe the person out after dark as shaded and obscured. This idea of being shrouded by the dark, of being unseen, excites emotions. We can see things, but no one can see us. We are hidden, spying out what is going on. The change of one's senses and sensibilities moving through darkness can be exciting—it's the feeling of seeing without being seen. Often, there is a sense of being self-contained and present. There is me, and then there is the otherness of the dark.

ESSAI 38
Palimpsest

The past is never dead. It is not even past.
—William Faulkner

From the 4th through 15th centuries, medieval scribes used parchment or vellum to create written documents, often religious texts. Parchment and vellum were writing surfaces sourced from animal skin, with parchment coming from goats and sheep, and vellum from calves (vellum and veal come from the same root word).

Parchment and vellum had two benefits for scribes. First, both endured the passage of time, unlike the more ancient papyrus, which was sourced from reeds and which crumbled with age. Second, scribes could reuse parchment and vellum, saving the cost of sourcing new hides and the effort of curing and cutting them to size. Reusing a piece of parchment involved a monk in a scriptorium scraping away the old text with a knife or with a pumice stone creating a clean surface on which a new document could be written.

In more modern times, as scholars examined the late medieval texts more closely, they found evidence of the older writing underneath. Many pre-11th-century undiscovered classic texts of Latin and Greek were found hidden beneath newer writing. Late Roman-era writings of mathematics, grammar, and law also came to light. Some original Greek versions of Bible passages and the Quran were discovered. Scholars labeled the hidden texts "palimpsests" from the greek "palin" (again) and "psestos" (scraped).

Use of word palimpsest has expanded over time to capture not just the manuscript definition, but the larger concept of a palimpsest as evidence of older times beneath or hidden by a modern sheen. In geomorphology, a landscape palimpsest would be evidence of older geologic structures representing quite different climatic conditions underneath or alongside current land development. In my neighborhood, there are boulder erratics (evidence of glaciation) resting on top of local sandstone (evidence of seas once covering the land) amidst upthrusts of basalt rock (evidence of long-past volcanic activity). Greenery and trees grow in topsoil, amidst glacial boulders and gravel, atop sandstone, and abutting basalt, creating a fascinating six-layer palimpsest of geo-ecological accumulation.

Architects and design historians also use the word palimpsest to describe the iteration of a design, a site, or a geographic area. Architecture and landscape development manifests through time, capturing history and leaving traces--the older buildings, the neighborhood schemes, the aged trees, and the shaped ground and turf. Each layer provides a window to the ideas and desires of an earlier era. Landscape historian John Stilgoe writes, "...a careful, confident explorer of the built environment soon sees all sorts of traces of past generations."

Identifying palimpsests is not only noteworthy but provides a more profound feeling of historicity and sacredness. In every town, physical markers offer a connection to the past, symbols of the temporal and spiritual roots of a community. Sometimes these markers are giant stones or trees. In Glen Rock, New Jersey, there is a giant boulder (the eponymous "Rock") that served as a geographic boundary in different town and county configurations over time. Now, the Rock is more of a village centerpiece with, not surprisingly, a plaque honoring local veterans. Until three years ago, Basking Ridge, New Jersey's giant White Oak lived for 600 years and represented an eye-stopping link to eras pre-nationhood, pre-colonial, and even pre-Columbian.

Finding remnants of old farms can trigger memories of pastoral idyll. Deep in some backyards, I espy pre-automobile horse barns, often with wood rotting away, but still sporting the oblong carriage doors and loft windows. Old New England stone walls, snaking through second-growth woods, signal the borders of prior farm fields or pastures. House foundations constructed from locally sourced stone indicate that the home might have originated as a farmhouse before being subsumed by suburban growth.

Local parks are often carved from old farmland, orchards, or in some cases, local estates. Some original farm and estate structures remain in palimpsest in parks today, especially outbuildings and old retaining walls. In my town, both the local art center and the community center reside in carriage houses of former estates. In a local park nearby, a pre-1900 stretch of sandstone blocks, originally a retaining wall for a large Victorian mansion, now partitions the kids' soccer field from the baseball diamond. Original iron fences and gates from the estate still mark the park's borders along the main road, and one can still trace the original driveway as a depression stretching across a grassy field.

Walking along streams, one finds palimpsest remnants of old mill dams where water from 1800s mill ponds still spill over small waterfalls. Encountering these ponds and dams, one can usually identify the placement of the old mill, which has since been torn down. One can explore on bike or foot for the source of streams or brooks and find fresh springs emerging from the ground in hidden glens behind suburban homes or shopping malls. We find shopping malls situated on what was formerly some of the least desired land pre-development. Large malls of suburban New Jersey can be found on low, marshy land unusable for farming. In my county, most of this land for a time lay at the bottom of glacial lakes. This land was still low-lying bog until drained in the 20th century for commerce. Behind many of the mall stores in my own Bergen County, one can still see marshy streams and stands of reeds.

Our downtowns are rife with palimpsests, as older homes and buildings sit cheek by jowl with modern structures. The Murray Hill section of New York City lies roughly between 32nd and 40th street in Midtown on the east side of Manhattan. The borders of Murray Hill are just an estimate because the New York street grid has over-written what once was a commanding hill with views both towards the East River and south to the old downtown. The geometry of the streets crossing at right angles has nearly erased the sense that the hill is even there. Unless one looks explicitly for the geologic palimpsest of the rise in elevation, it is difficult to sense any discontinuity in the land. At first, Murray Hill developed as a place for upscale mansions, most notably as the residence of financier J.P. Morgan, given the desirability of the hill's views and breezes. With the development of the city, the spread of modern office high-rises on Madison and Park Avenues subsumed many of these structures. Discovering the hill and its original buildings becomes a treasure hunt.

Another palimpsest example, further south in the city, is Union Square, which lies at the crossing of 14th street, Broadway, and Park Avenue South. Redesigned in the 1980s, Union Square retains original 19th-century elements of curving paths and gardens as well as statues of Washington, Lincoln, and Lafayette (the park originated in 1839). One palimpsest that I found particularly fascinating involves buildings that border the park. At the southeast corner on 14th street, stand the Zeckendorf Towers, a four finial apartment complex built in 1987 on the site of the old Klein's department store. A bit further east, behind the old Klein's and now behind the new towers, one finds the Consolidated Edison Company Building, constructed in 1926. A colossal clock sat atop the ConEd building and still does. From 1926-1987, sojourners in Union Square could look up at the grand clock and note the time. With the construction of the Zeckendorf Towers, though, the 1926 clock was blocked from view, receding in palimpsest to the more modern building in front. Like a medieval scholar, one can still spot the clock by moving to a specific location in the park, where the clock face becomes visible as it peers almost shyly between two of the apartment blocks.

The English essayist and social critic Thomas De Quincey (1785-1859) penned an article titled, "The Palimpsest of the Human Brain." In it, he extols the virtues of the palimpsest as an intellectual dialectic:

> *What would you think, fair reader, of a problem such as this,—to write a book which should be sense for your own generation, nonsense for the next, should revive into sense for the next after that, but again become nonsense for the fourth; and so on by alternate successions, sinking into night or blazing into day.*

De Quincey notes how a piece of classic learning is scraped away to write a monastic tome, which is then scraped for the scribing of an Arthurian legend, following which an enlightenment scholar detects the original classic palimpsest, recovers the original masterpiece, and celebrates its learning. De Quincy goes further:

Michael Faherty

*What else than a natural and mighty palimpsest is the
human brain? Such a palimpsest is my brain; such a
palimpsest, oh reader! is yours. Everlasting layers of ideas,
images, feelings, have fallen upon your brain softly as
light. Each succession has seemed to bury all that went
before. And yet, in reality, not one has been extinguished.
...countless are the mysterious hand-writings of grief or
joy which have inscribed themselves successively upon
the palimpsest of your brain; and, like the annual leaves
of aboriginal forests, or the undissolving snows on the
Himalaya, or light falling upon light.*

Here, De Quincy captures the larger truth that palimpsests
in whatever manifestation—literary, geological, architectural,
or biological— are the reflection of time and accumulation.
The accumulation of palimpsests is less about the new covering
and hiding the old, but more about building something more
exceptional. Layer by layer, year by year, idea on top of idea,
we and the world evolve in growth, and we should cherish the
old with the new.

ESSAI 39
Myths

"God what an outfield," he says. ... He looks up
at me, and I look down at him. "This must be
heaven," he says.
"No. It's Iowa."

—W. P. Kinsella, "Shoeless Joe"

What is it about the sight of a field--a baseball diamond, a stand of corn, a broad stretch of parkland--that triggers a kind of nostalgia? Is there something deep in our amygdala that craves a rural view, a sense of the farm?

I remember a corn field behind the house where I lived on Long Island back in the 1970s. Our home was in a suburb, one that was not that far from New York City, but back then, farms and homes coexisted side by side more often than now. My parents' manicured lawn and well-weeded flower beds rested a stone's throw from a farmer's cornfield. With my brothers and sisters, I would go back into the field and steal some ears, bringing them home for dinner. There was something elemental in that we could venture out of our backyard into a rural idyll. Back then as kids, we shucked corn, picked straw-berries, mowed the lawn, weeded Mom's vegetable garden, and visited the pumpkin patch. These were all small ways that we stayed in touch with an innate farm spirit. For me, the sense of farmland and farming triggers the nostalgia both of boyhood and something primal about history, nature, and the passing of time.

I get this same feeling of nostalgia from small-town main streets. Our mind's eye conjures the row of businesses—the hardware store and the scoop shop, the drugstore and the delicatessen, the post office and the local theater, the bank and the railroad station—all with turn of the century architecture, fronted by a wide sidewalk with strolling pedestrians. Walt Disney created an idealized small town with the "Main Street U.S.A." section in his Disney theme parks. Based on his hometown of Marceline, Missouri, Disney sought to capture something universal about the town square and main street of shops, embedding an iconography of Americana. Other examples abound:

- Greenfield Village in Dearborn, Michigan is an outdoor history museum designed as a small, historic town.
- Colonial Williamsburg seeks to recreate a colonial-era crafts village.
- Retirement communities erect faux town squares and shops reminiscent of an idealized 1950s.

In our films, small-town main streets and squares represent purity of time and spirit. Think of the uncorrupted perfection of Hill Valley of 1955 in "Back to the Future," Bedford Falls in "It's a Wonderful Life," and Mayberry in the "Andy Griffith Show."

During the mid-20th century, nostalgia for old farms and small-towns became an intellectual cause célèbre with writing and art delving into themes of authenticity and an idealized past. In the 1950s, the artist Eric Sloane wrote a series of books about the vanishing of the rural landscape, celebrating 1800s Americana and its values. In his book, *America Yesterday*, Sloane calls out, "It is important to remember, when comparing the past with the present, not to allow modern wonders to awe one into believing that all changes are synonymous with progress." Sloane celebrated the past, writing another of his books:

> *The pattern of our early landscape was capacious and orderly. Its texture, which were the people and their farms, had the mellowness and dignity of well-seasoned wood. Close at hand there were lanes with vaulting canopies of trees and among them were houses with personalities like human beings. At a distance it was all a patchwork quilt of farm plots sewn together with rough black stitching of stone fences.*

Romanticizing the landscape, Sloane levers analogies from nature and religion while calling forth homespun history. He uses his formidable drawing skills to depict in detail the elements of the landscape that have disappeared, recapturing them for us. In one book, Sloane draws three different types of canal boats, seven different types of mills, and nine variations of sleds. In other books, he details in words and pictures types of barns, weathervanes, and covered bridges. Sloane is not just showing us what has gone before, but also how those things worked effectively back then. He pines for the practicality of the past and celebrates the discoveries he makes.

I believe that we share a universal longing for historic landscapes linked to the myth of an American pre-industrial past--the belief that our land before the 20th century, comprised of farms, mills, seaports, schoolhouses, and small towns, was somehow better than it currently is. We see small-town and rural life as more straightforward, with values and beliefs that are purer, more grounded, and more authentic than what we have in the complex, modern, industrialized world today.

This belief in the rural myth is a reaction to the stress

of industrialization and the loss of independence that many Americans still feel as workers entombed in companies and organizations. Deep down, we feel we have forsaken the freedom of the pastoral landscape for the constrictions of modern culture, leading to this idealization of the past. Escaping the city to see fall foliage, recreating the feel of New England villages in outdoor malls, and conserving older homes with historic landmark status are all symptomatic of the desire to return to a mythical America. We know factually that our heritage is not pure, but the old landscape and architectural forms have emotional leverage. Our modern sensibility of machines, technology, data, and communications desires deeper resonance with past, with purer American forms.

ESSAI 40
The Villa Lante

When I investigate and when I discover that
the forces of the heavens and the planets are
within ourselves, then truly I seem to be living
among the gods.

—*Leon Battista Alberti*

In the summer of 1991, I took a bus from Rome northwards to
the small village of Bagnaia three miles to the east of the town
of Viterbo in central Italy. Bagnaia is home to the Villa Lante,
a 16th-century country house and garden designed by the
architect Giacoma da Vignolo for Cardinal Francesco Gambara.

The fame of the Villa Lante lies in its large Renaissance
garden that flows from the back of the villa house atop a hill,
downwards towards the little village of Bagnaia. The garden
features structures and sculptures replete with classical and
biblical themes as well as a variety of channels and fountains that
pour and spout water creating intrigue and surprise. There are
two parts to the garden: the garden proper--a series of minutely
architected terraces bisected by running water and featuring a
central water element—and lower down, a surrounding bosco
(wooded park) which suggests a more ancient wilderness ideal
with its trees, diagonal pathways, and seeming haphazard
placement of sculpture.

At the Villa Lante design rises to the level of art. Here we see the idea of the garden as a third conception of nature. If we designate untouched wilderness as the first type of nature, and pastoral farm or grazing lands as the next level, then the Villa Lante represents something different. Villa Lante is an artistic recreation of an ideal—neither wild nor utilitarian— but an imagined reprise of Eden where the harmony of nature and man is reestablished and bliss is pursued. It is a garden comprised of natural and architectural forms designed to entertain, instruct, and elicit reverence.

The wonder of the Villa Lante is the integration of two themes, order and wilderness, into an integrated whole. The garden can be viewed in its entirety from two vantage points, reflecting the hill venue. One can look upwards at terraced gardens topped by the grand villa at the start of the journey from the park at the bottom of the hill, or one can turn and look downwards from the villa at the end of the journey, surveying the terraces and park from above. From these vantage points, the garden takes on the appearance of a painting inscribed on the hillside. One can contemplate the journey from the woods into the more formal design and home above, or look backward at the journey just made, from arboreal to humanistic. In a way, this reflects our life journeys from the wildness of youth to the gained perspective of old age. We immerse ourselves in life, only intermittently stepping back, seeking a fuller view, and ascribing meaning.

The formal garden of Villa Lante entertains us and tells a story. One first enters the garden from the wooded bosco at the lower terrace and then proceeds from there to the top. Representing the extremity of order, the lower terrace consists of 12 gardens bordered by boxwoods surrounding a water parterre. The entire terrace is a study in geometry with its quadrilateral symmetry and imposition of circles and squares.

This terrace is a sharp counterpoint to the more wild woods just left behind.

One then can proceed from this lower garden upward via a succession of terraces and fountains to the top of the hill. Each terrace and fountain has a different theme. There is the Fountain of Lights, the Fountain of Dolphins, the Fountain of the River Gods, and the Fountain of the Deluge. Each fountain provided entertainment through its design or surprise jets of water.

Throughout the journey, one walks or climbs steps beside a central axis of running water, which proceeds from fountain to fountain. Each tier of the garden is compartmentalized and designed with a specific meaning. One can contrast the large, classical, partitioned, and tranquil fountain of the lower level, with the Etruscan motifs in the Fountain of the Dolphins in the next tier, and then with the riotous spouts of the Fountain of the River Gods on the third tier. As we proceed through the garden, we are moving back in time from Roman to Etruscan to the time of the gods, and as we do so, the water in the successive fountains moves from placid to more wild. The garden culminates with the Fountain of the Deluge, which reprises the great flood via its waterfalls. Within the garden, we are thus exposed to classic geometry, Romanesque sculpture, Greek myth, and biblical stories. The garden elicits emotion from the exertion of the climb and the varied themes, while also providing a deeper sense of the continuity of history. The stream of water flows from the top of the hill through the diverse garden elements. The seriousness of the themes is leavened by the delight in surprise water spouts and the crayfish motif, which appears throughout. A crayfish in Italian is a "gambera," which is a play on the name of Cardinal Gambara, who commissioned the garden design for his home.

Beyond the everyday of the landscape around us such as the

roads, baseball fields or main streets, and beyond the natural elements that we see like the fields, mountains, or forests, we see with the Villa Lante that the design of the land can accede to something more--a higher state. Landscape can equal art, equivalent to the intent and beauty of a painting or a sculpture. Landscape can touch our souls. We can experience the feeling of a designed piece of land, intellectually and emotionally, and delve into the designer's intent and the provenance of the form.

ESSAI 41
Lawn

Americans devote 70 hours annually, to pushing petrol-powered spinning death blades over aggressively pointless green carpets to meet an embarrassingly destructive beauty standard based on specious homogeneity.

—*Ian Graber-Stiehl*

Lawns cover 40 million acres in the United States, the equivalent of 18 Yellowstone parks. They are the largest irrigated crop in the country, with municipalities devoting almost half of their water use in support. Lawns consume 70 million pounds of fertilizer each year. This fertilizer requires 2X volume of fossil fuel to create 1X nitrogen (the critical component of fertilizer). The conversion of natural gas to nitrogen fertilizer for lawns leads to 70,000 tons of CO_2 emissions per annum. Seventy-eight million homes in the United States use lawn pesticides. Lawn pesticides are used at 2X the rate of pesticides on food crops. Manufacturers sell about five million lawnmowers per year to maintain the national lawn-scape. Lawnmowers use over 500 million gallons of gas and emit five and a half million tons of carbon dioxide yearly into the atmosphere. Leaf-blowers add to this total. Lawnmowers and leaf-blowers both operate above 70 decibels, beyond the considered safe level of 55. Just listen to the machining of your neighborhood on any weekday. That is the death toll of us wasting water to create biological deserts that contribute to global warming so we can enjoy a meaningless 19th century aesthetic.

I am admittedly at fault here. Lawns cover 20% of the land in the state of New Jersey, and my home half-acre contributes to this statistic. I pay for a crew to fertilize and de-weed the lawn four times a year and cut the grass weekly from April to October. In a way, I am afraid not to have a lawn. What would the neighbors think? In our American mind's eye we have an ideal suburban template of beauty consisting of a house surrounded by green, bordered by shrubs and mulched gardens, with intermittent trees. I now know this isn't right and that I have to do something.

Lawns have devolved over time. The original word derived from Old French was "laund" which referred to a glade or opening in a forest. From Shakespeare in *Henry VI*, we get the sense of a "laund" as a place of adventure, embedded in a surrounding wood: "Under this thick-grown brake we'll shroud ourselves, For through this laund anon the deer will come." In the 17th century, the word evolved to "lawn" suggesting less a forest opening and more a stretch of untilled ground where sheep might be tended. In the next century, we see the change in meaning towards more formal and tended spaces, as lawns became a design element in more extensive gardens. The royal garden at Versailles near Paris used the "tapis verte" (green carpet) as a design element for its parterres. In the English Landscape tradition, the architect Capability Brown featured sweeps of greensward in his designs. Later, the designer Humphrey Repton created "Home Lawns" as more formal green-space near the mansion houses for cricket. Early in the 19th century, Thomas Jefferson labeled his green quadrangle at the University of Virginia as "The Lawn," and lawns have become the primary landscape of college quads since. Village greens, which were originally common town land for sheep or cattle grazing, transformed more into parks for lounging or sports. The Dartmouth Green in Hanover, New Hampshire, served the dual purpose of college quadrangle and town green.

Lawns thus evolved from mere forest meadows to untilled pastoral land, then to formal garden elements, and more broadly to quads and town greens. Central Park in New York City captures nearly all of these lawn elements. The original park design featured "The Mall" bordered with grassy parterres, "The Green" initially designed for grazing sheep, the rolling "North Meadow," the "Ball Ground" for recreation, and "The Ramble" with intermittent glades amidst wooded paths. Later, the "Great Lawn" was built, taking the place of the old Croton Reservoir and serving as a central place for recreation and concerts. Whether it is the delightful view of a grassy meadow expanse, the resonance of a pastoral scene, the surprise in emerging into a gap in the forest, or the joy of recreational sports, these varied expressions of the lawn in Central Park reflect the different sensibilities we have about open spaces and their different uses. Importantly, the variety of the landscape in Central Park with woods, meadows, flower beds, and tended lawns creates a more balanced template in its conception and care of nature.

By the mid-nineteenth century, lawn designs were still relegated to private estates, public parks, and universities. The affordability of large untilled parcels and the cost of their maintenance prohibited more widespread ownership. The middle and lower classes could not own lawns themselves until it became cheaper to do so. Four elements converged to facilitate the extensive use of the suburban lawns that we know today. First, land ownership outside urban areas became viable with the growth of railroad towns and villages commutable to the central metropolitan area. These new towns made land ownership accessible and affordable. Second, the aesthetic of the stand-alone country house or cottage with the surrounding garden, which began with the writings of Andrew Jackson Downing in the 1840s, emerged as the desired form. Third, the lawnmower and eventually the motorized lawnmower allowed the less wealthy homeowner to tend their lawns in reasonable time with less effort, changing the lawn maintenance value equation (scything was brutal work and time consuming).

The final enabler of suburban lawn sprawl was the imposition of town codes regarding landscaping, which dictated that homes must have tended lawns and gardens. These codes--combined with unstated but real community pressure around maintaining home values through home and landscape uniformity--led to what we see today. Many towns in the East and Northeast of the United States adhere to rules codified by BOCA: the Building Officials and Code Administrators International. The name itself has a Big Brother feel, suggesting a lock-step approach to town development. BOCA dictates the following: "All premises and exterior property shall be maintained free from weeds or plant growth in excess of 10 inches (254mm). All noxious weeds shall be prohibited. Weeds shall be defined as all grasses, annual plants and vegetation, other than trees or shrubs provided; however, this term shall not include cultivated flowers and gardens."

The implications of this are clear: one cannot allow weeds (e.g., wild grasses or wildflowers); grass must be cut; and flower gardens, shrubs, and trees are encouraged. My town adheres to BOCA, and the local Director of Building and Inspections is allowed, after a written notice and ten-day period, to come onto one's property to remove weeds (or tree stumps, or trash). The town bylaws are clear what's at stake: "the appearance of the premises and structures shall not constitute a blighting factor for adjoining property owners nor an element leading to the progressive deterioration and downgrading of the neighborhood with the accompanying diminution of property values."

Here we see economic greed trumping ecologic need, with a green tyranny that is both stultifying in its uniformity and immoral in its effects. As stated, the environmental consequences of our lawns include carbon emissions, noise pollution, use of pesticides, and reduction in animal life. Critically, lawns do a deficient job trapping carbon and managing water runoff, relative to trees and meadows. The decline in fauna is especially troublesome: the last 30 years have seen the diminution of bee colonies, especially the native bumblebee, with some estimates around 90%. Bees are critical for pollination and thus the sustenance of plant species. Separately, bird populations have been impacted by the reduction in food sources like caterpillars, which require more native forest-like environments and ground cover to survive.

Doug Tallamy, in his book *Nature's Best Hope*, asks us to take some simple steps to reduce the environmental impact of our lawns. He suggests shrinking our lawns, taking half of the space, and replanting it with native keystone trees like white oak, cherry, or willow, creating a grove ideally with some ground cover of rocks, logs, shrubs, and even leaf litter. Tallamy further advocates planting stands of pollinators such as sunflowers, goldenrods, or blueberries to facilitate the return of bees. I remember a field in back of our house when I was a kid, which was replete with goldenrod and flush with thousands of bees each year. Tallamy cites New York's High Line park's success, which features extensive wildflower plantings, celebrating a less-ordered, more elemental gardening style. Importantly, Tallamy threads the needle of local bylaws, as he does not recommend letting weeds run rampant and the complete elimination of the lawns, but instead advocates having reduced lawn areas, well-trimmed, as borders for more wild areas. If one conceives and maintains a new grove of trees or a stand of sunflowers as a different type of garden that is confined to a specific area of the yard, one is likely adhering to local landscape code.

I think the result of having more variety in our local properties is a landscape that is inherently more satisfying. The experience of a grove of trees opening on a glade of lawn can return us to the original conception of a lawn as an opening in the woods. A bed of wildflower, a bit run amok, can be just as beautiful as an ordered row of tulips. We can still retain formal garden elements, we can still enjoy lawn for sport, but we can also recognize that we have a larger responsibility to have less of an impact on the natural world.

ESSAI 42
Solitude and Meditation

The nurse of full grown souls is solitude
—James Russell Lowell

Sometime around 500 B.C., Siddhartha Gautama, at the age of 35, sat down under a pipal tree in northern India and remained there for 48 days meditating, forsaking his friends and all contact with the world around him. On the 49th day, Gautama achieved "enlightenment"—an awakening to the truths of the causes of human suffering and the path one must take to achieve nirvana. When we think of meditation, we often conjure the image of the Buddha. The Buddha sits serene, lotus style, seeking enlightenment, focused not on the outer world but on the calm and peace of the true inner self. The Buddha becomes fully present and aware in the moment, as meditation becomes a way of being in the world divorced from the tension of exigency or strife.

Whether it is with the Buddha and his tree, Jesus during his 40 days, Moses climbing Mount Sinai, Confucius's three years of mourning, or Mohammed and his cave, religious texts proscribe solitude as a universal path to revelation. Michel de Montaigne wrote, "Wherefore it is not enough to have gotten away from the crowd, it is not enough to move; we must get away from the gregarious instincts that are inside us, we must sequester ourselves and repossess ourselves." Through solitude, Montaigne believes, we re-establish the relationship with self as the basis for anything that might come next: "Here our ordinary conversation must be between us and ourselves, and so private that no outside association or communication can find a place." In solitude we enable ourselves to renounce the cacophony of everyday concerns and simply let the world be. Ralph Waldo Emerson wrote, "great genial power... consists in not being original at all,—in being altogether receptive; in letting the world do all, and suffering the spirit of the hour to pass unobstructed through the mind." The Christian theologian, Thomas Merton, adds, "there is greater comfort in the substance of silence than in the answer to a question."

Often solitude is experienced while immersed in nature-- under a tree, on a mountain, in a cave or desert. We venture from our homes to divorce ourselves from the mental baggage of the quotidian. Natural forms provide a calming antidote. Jean Jacques Rousseau wrote, "never have I been so much myself ... as in the journeys I have taken alone and on foot." Author and environmentalist Wendell Berry talks of his hikes: "I can move without reference to anything other than the lay of the land and the capabilities of my own body. The necessities of foot travel have stripped away all superfluities. I am reduced to my irreducible self." Berry calls out the need to shed the accouterments of society and ego, to see and understand just the essentials. Berry writes: "I come to nature to enact the loneliness and humbleness of my kind ... to accept a humbler and truer view of myself than I usually have." Nature is a bulwark against which we find our humble measure as simple, transparent, and ephemeral.

Wes spend most of our lives in an endless, self-centered mental dialogue. Our roving brains grab onto circumstances and create fanciful meanings and false emotions. We create an ever-shifting world between our two ears of thoughts and interpretation, happiness and misery, action and result. We give little time to standing back and stopping the flow, despite how critically important it is. Going outside can be surcease.

Thirteen million Americans talk a walk every day. These folks see walking as a way to stay fit, as a way to connect with friends, and as a way to stay emotionally healthy. They have grasped an essential notion about life. They understand that life is not always about the rush, not about the extremes, but about the ability to stay centered amidst the flux and stress of what happens daily. They understand, even if it is not always top of mind, what it means to get in touch with their true selves, their physical self and their psychological self, to achieve a holistic equanimity.

For many Americans, walking is their version of meditation. Noted author and professor John Kabat-Zinn writes, "Meditation is the only intentional, systematic human activity which at bottom is about not trying to improve yourself ... but simply to realize where you already are." The classic meditation path is one of sitting and stillness, but, there are advocates of the walking meditation as well. The 20th century Buddhist teacher Thich Nhat Hanh writes: "When you practice walking meditation, you go for a stroll. You have no purpose or direction in space or time. The purpose of walking meditation is walking meditation itself. Going is important, not arriving. Walking meditation is not a means to an end; it is an end."

There are different approaches to doing a walking meditation, but they all start with setting a cadence, one that is unrushed and deliberate. One begins by merely counting steps, setting a mental rhythm that is initially just physical. First, note the impact of your steps on the bottom of your feet, then the sensation of your ankles flexing, followed by your calves, then your knees, then your quadriceps, hamstrings, and glutes. One can feel the swing of the legs back and forth. With the rhythm established, you can then turn inward and take inventory of thoughts or emotions, noting them but not dwelling on them. Let these thoughts go and focus on the body as a whole moving as a unit down the sidewalk, street, or path. If something distracts you—a car, a bird, or a street sign—note it and then return your focus to the action of the steps and perhaps also the swinging of your arms.

We gain personal freedom by taking back possession of the present moment. All of us face issues and concerns that capture our minds and bodies, removing us from what is around us. Wendell Berry wrote, "Though I am here in my body, my mind and nerves too are not yet altogether here." Regaining a sense of self is not easy, but returning to nature and going back out into the world of sky, hills, and fields can be a start on the right path.

ESSAI 43
Right of Way

Towering genius disdains a beaten path. It seeks regions hitherto unexplored.

—Abraham Lincoln

From the age of 9 to 15, I lived in the village of Lloyd Harbor on the north shore of Long Island. My Uncle Walter, who lived close by, would take us kids on long walks through the woods and fields behind our house. We lived at that time in a new housing development, and behind us stretched a large cornfield, and behind that lay mostly empty tracts of land owned by the Catholic Church for a diocesan seminary. Beyond that, the Quakers had taken over an old estate and made it into a small college. It was a holy wildness as the land had once been developed, but large swathes had fallen mostly into disuse.

Uncle Walter was cool because he knew stuff, and he was skinny, wore work boots, and sported a 1970s blonde curly beard. I remember him showing us how to spot wild onions. When he first did this, he bent over and pulled up the plant, rubbed the dirt off the onion root, and ate it. He was a poison-ivy savant too, able to spot the sinister, shiny three-leaved evil and warn us away. He had patience with us kids, and he knew that he could help his sister by taking us away from the house for a while for an experience beyond the manicured lawn and cement patio.

On these Uncle Walter hikes, we discovered all sorts of strangeness. Once, we came across a house that had collapsed. There was no sign of the wreckage being removed, just boards, and nails, and plaster, and plumbing all jumbled in a heap. It was as if an oblivious giant had stomped on the home and then just continued walking.

Another time we came across a series of overgrown ponds, descending in tiers down a hillside. We wondered what they could be for. Maybe fisheries? There was the day that we walked down to the Quaker college and out onto the harbor beach behind the main building. It was the 1970s, and the college students all were "hippies," at least that's what my parents said. Down at the beach, we spotted a naked couple skinny dipping. Uncle Walter turned us around quickly.

And then there was the time when we found the shell middens. A shell midden is a mound of dirt and shells that indicates that Native Americans once lived nearby. Uncle Walter explained to us how shellfish were a primary source of food back then and that the middens were basically refuse heaps. I learned later that my uncle was an actual authority on locations of Native American shell middens on Long Island. A local newspaper article praised him for keeping many of the locations secret to ensure they would not be disturbed.

In our neighborhood, we often spotted pheasants popping out of hedges or woods. These pheasants were not native, but the remnants of birds originally stocked by Marshall Field III for bird hunts at his Gold Coast estate nearby that he built in the 1920s. Just like the pheasants, we willingly crossed property and boundaries on our walks, understanding and a little bit thrilled by the fact that we were trespassing. We just walked and explored.

I was 11 then, and I was free: free to walk with my uncle; free to walk on my own to the beach, following local bridle paths; free to bike ride to the town of Huntington three miles away for candy and pizza with friends; free to read what I wanted to. If I could chart "freedom" on a graph, with "degrees of free'ness" on the y-axis, and my age along the x-axis, I think freedom peaked for me at age 11.

Kids often ignore private property and boundaries as they wander. There is a sense of adventure to get off pavement and cut behind houses, across fields, and through the woods. So many of our childhood books feature just this sort of wandering. In the Harry Potter books, Harry and his friends often steal into the Forbidden Forest, where things are strange (unicorns, centaurs, and Hagrid with his creatures). Frodo, Sam, and Pippin cut through the hedge and across fields at the start of their quest in *The Lord of the Rings*, eschewing the road and later trespassing on Farmer Maggot's farm trying to take a short cut. In *The Secret Garden*, Mary Lennox crosses the Missel Moor, befriends the boy Dicken who has a deep understanding of nature and the moor. Mary then finds a key to a hidden and forbidden garden. And in *Watership Down*, Hazel and his rabbit companions go on a quest across the countryside, over a river, cutting through a village green and different farms before arriving at the large hill where they make their new home.

There is a youthful presumption of the idea of "right of way"--of the ability to cut across the land on footpaths or bridleways. The United Kingdom passed a law in 2000 called the "Countryside and Rights of Way Act" which put into law the 'right to roam' on "mountain, moor, heath, and down" as well as common lands in England. The law confirms what Englanders had been doing for centuries, and what I did as an 11-year-old, which is hiking on paths across private but undeveloped land. The law codifies the idea that walking, or "roaming," was a right that could not be trumped by property ownership and that undeveloped land belonged to the people. The law also imposes a responsibility on the walker to respect the land—something Uncle Walter exemplified, too—precluding damage of any "any wall, fence, hedge, stile, or gate."

I wish we had this law in the United States. Right of way in here often refers to the government having authority to build roads across property. We are "free" in America, but not truly free as individuals to go where we want. Too often, law and life erect a sign that says, "No Trespassing." We struggle to break through the barrier.

I retain something of my 11-year-old self to this day. When I walk around the town where I live now, I enjoy cutting behind, through, or across rather than sticking to straight sidewalks. In a nearby park, I often venture with my dog out of the park proper, cutting behind a 150-year-old barn and along the path where old train tracks once ran. There was another old railway on the other side of town, too, that was built early in the 1900s but is now removed, where one can still follow the route it made cutting behind houses and schools, and across newly built parking lots. Off of a dead-end street a few blocks away, one can find a trail that cuts through woodland and along a stream before emerging across the town border. And in our town proper, one can cut through behind stores and backlots, where you can get a glimpse of the small apartments, store sheds, and employee hangouts. It's like peaking backstage at how a performance operates.

There is a delight in getting off the beaten path, in the exploration of something hidden, in discovering new truths. Having the "right of way" across the land, the ability to trek and explore feels to me an ultimate expression of what it means to be human. Our minds are geared to curiosity, and our legs are evolved to walking distances over variable terrain. We are of unconstrained design. The attitude of the explorer feels right—an expression of our life, our freedom, and clearly a pursuit of happiness. As such, we should treat right of way as the inalienable right it is and reopen the land to our walks.

ESSAIESSAY 44
Wordsworth

Oft on the dappled turf at ease; I sit and play with similes.

— *William Wordsworth*

The poet William Wordsworth and his sister Dorothy, and sometimes their friend and fellow poet Samuel Coleridge, often took long hikes across the countryside in northern and western England. In 1898, Wordsworth set out from Bristol and crossed the Severn River on a ferry to alight in Wales. He then walked 10 miles through the countryside to visit the ruins of Tintern Abbey. From this visit (and from prior unrecorded ones as well), he devised his great Romantic poem: "Composed a few miles above Tintern Abbey, on revisiting the Banks of the Wye,"

Back in the day, our teachers explained the significance of different historical eras like the Classical, Medieval, Renaissance, Enlightenment, Baroque, Neo-Classical, Modern, and even the Post-Modern. The one period that always struck me funny was the Romantic era. Naively, I equated the Romantic with "romance," as in romance novels, and perhaps a kind of a Jane Austen'ish take on society. The Romantic era seemed an outlier in the linear progress of the arts and sciences, from the humanistic base of the Renaissance, through the Enlightenment's growing rationalism, followed by the science of the Industrial Revolution, to our own modern era. Recently, though, I've come to appreciate the thinkers and writers of the Romantic period.

Stretching from the late 18th towards the mid-19th century, the Romantic era can be seen as a reaction to the reason and rationality of the Enlightenment and Neo-classicism. I think of it now as a cultural turning back inward to reestablish the basis of the individual and the soul amidst the changing world. This cultural stream has proved both enduring and critical since then. There is a Romantic sensibility that can resonate today as we retain this need to look inside ourselves to find meaning.

Wordsworth's life and poetics were an exemplar of the Romantic movement in literature, philosophy, and art. Romanticism, at its core, was a celebration of the individual, and one's individual sensibility. As a reaction to the elitism of the Enlightenment and Classicism, it returned to the values of everyday people, regional and national culture, and connection with nature.

In Romanticism, sincerity and simplicity trumped pretense and complexity. Fads and fashion gave way to reality and forthrightness. The 18th French philosopher, Jean Jacques Rousseau, wrote about the need to return to one's "natural" state and to regain independence of thought and action from the dictates of civil society. In a natural state, morals and virtue would supersede commerce and false society. Rousseau put forth a call to action:

> *Exalted by these sublime meditations my soul soared towards Divinity, from whose height I looked down on my fellow men pursuing the blind path of their prejudices, of their errors, of their misfortunes and their crimes. Then I cried to them in a voice which they could not hear,*

Michael Faherty

'Madmen who ceaselessly complain … learn that all your misfortunes arise from yourselves!'

Rousseau is asking for both a transcendence above the petty foibles and concerns in which we become mired, as well as a return to a more simple, pure, and even naive state of nature. We see this also in the character of Goethe's Faust, who struggles with the choice of material pleasure versus divine contemplation and acceptance. Both Rousseau and Goethe sensed the potential tragedy of the modern world, seducing and blinding us with materiality. They both also raised the prospect of salvation through nature.

Wordsworth picks up these Romantic themes, elucidating the desire for harmony and oneness between the individual and nature. At Tintern Abbey, Wordsworth writes that he was:

…well pleased to recognize
In nature and the language of the sense
The anchor of my purest thoughts, the nurse,
The guide, the guardian of my heart, and soul
Of all my moral being.

Nature anchors Wordsworth--nurses him, guides him, and guards his heart and soul. The grandeur and sublime of nature renew the sense of self for Wordsworth. He writes of the resonance of landscape forms:

…in lonely rooms, and 'mid the din
Of towns and cities, I have owed to them
In hours of weariness, sensations sweet,
Felt in the blood, and felt along the heart;
And passing even into my purer mind,
With tranquil restoration.

During times of loneliness, amidst the noisiness of life, when he was weary, Wordsworth's memory of the landscape creates sensation which flows from the senses through the body to the heart and mind, restoring him. Tintern Abbey was a return to a place he remembered from years past. It is the remembrance of youthful freedom brought forth with redemptive power to the present. The future is made more serene as the mind now has refreshed memories to draw upon. Wordsworth's nature prescription nurtures heart and soul.

For all of us, it is a practical prescription of how to take the sublime and perhaps make it part of the every day. Wordsworth identifies the sublime in nature as:

> *A presence that disturbs me with the joy*
> *Of elevated thoughts: a sense sublime*
> *Of something far more deeply interfused...*
> *A motion and a spirit that impels*
> *All thinking things, all objects of all thought.*

A conception of nature as immanent, filled with something holy, became a core Romantic idea that echoed into 19th century philosophy, painting, and social movements. Even at the start of the industrial age, we see that the individual's role remained paramount. The idea of a man or woman humble before nature (often before god) established itself as a counterpoint to the dehumanization of modernization. This was the great gift of the Romantic movement that it established a countercurrent of the self which has persisted to this day and on which we can draw.

ESSAI 45
Emerson

I love the picturesque glitter of a summer morning's landscape. It kindles this burning admiration of nature and enthusiasm of mind."

—*Ralph Waldo Emerson*

What is the reason to ruminate on landscape, nature, philosophy, and literature? I believe deeply that part of our purpose in the world is to get in touch frequently with things above and beyond the everyday, to transcend our circumstances. Perhaps initially, we try to do this through career, family, and the accumulation of possessions. Sometimes we focus on social issues, community, or government. I think, though, that it is through our own intellectual and spiritual development that we can best enable transcendence, that it is more through the personal acquisition of knowledge, experience, and emotional scope, separate from the outward accouterments of success, that we rise higher.

The Latin root "scend" means to climb and can be found in many of our modern English words. Our word "ascend" mirrors the Latin verb "ascendere" (to climb up), and the word "scenic" suggests a view of the land available after the climb is made. "Transcend" would, therefore, offer the idea of climbing over or perhaps climbing across; however, this word has taken on a more spiritual meaning. We use the term to signal a moving above and beyond the self and everyday concerns. One who transcends a matter perceives an issue at a higher level with more perspective, perhaps then leaving that concern behind.

Transcendentalism emerged as an intellectual movement in New England in the 1840s. Led by author, poet, and orator Ralph Waldo Emerson, Transcendentalists believed the revelation of truth and divinity emanates from the insight of the individual. Meaning emerges internally and intuitively. Emerson wrote, "Self-knowledge and self-cultivation is not a means to something but the end—the goal of life itself." Self-realization precedes and supersedes social construct. Individual autonomy and freedom become coupled with the intuitive sense of right and wrong, and thus Transcendentalism inspires ethical behavior, a self-derived morality, and passion for rightness and advocacy.

For Transcendentalists, self-learning and self-knowledge inspire a deep connection to the spiritual nature of the world. Emerson writes, "Let a man not resist the law of his mind and he will be filled with the divinity that flows through all things." It is this individual link with divinity that Emerson called out as transcendence, a going beyond the limits of self to a larger connection.

For Emerson, transcendence begins with an assertion of self and a call to freedom:

I am solitary in the vast society of beings ... I am in the midst of them, but not of them; I hear the song of the storm ... I see cities and nations and witness passions ... but I partake it not.... .

Who is he that shall control me? Why may I not act and speak and write and think with entire freedom? What am I to the universe, or, the universe, what is it to me? Who hath forged the chains of wrong and right, of Opinion and Custom? And must I wear them?

Emerson lived in Concord, Massachusetts, famed for its role at the outset of the American Revolution and uniquely placed close to the intellectual center of Boston. Concord existed at the confluence of small-town simplicity, metropolitan adjacency, and accessibility to nature. Emerson and his colleagues, especially his intellectual offspring Henry David Thoreau, spent time walking from the town into an evolving landscape consisting of farmland, rocky outcroppings, millponds, railroad cuts, meadows, and woodlots. One senses in their writing the duality of being out in nature combined with the scribe's imperative: they wrote down their observations of nature and the added thoughts and especially feelings that nature triggered. For Emerson and his cohort, nature became both the inspiration and the metaphor for spiritual life:

The happiest man is he who learns from nature the lesson of worship.

... the exercise of all the senses is as intense pleasure, as anyone will find.

... the noblest ministry of nature is to stand as the apparition of God. It is the organ through which the universal spirit speaks to the individual, and strives to lead back the individual to it.

Let a man not resist the law of his mind and he will be filled with the divinity that flows through all things.

The intensity and pleasure of nature were more than just an admiration of an aesthetic. The Transcendentalists searched for discontinuity in nature, a grandeur that was rough and untamed. Nature was something to be analyzed and categorized with reason and curiosity to determine its actual components.

In this more authentic real nature, one moves beyond simple beauty to detect the sublime--the presence of a broader spirit in the world. This spirit was both complex and persistent, beyond the compass of man in time and meaning. Transcendentalists saw the nature experience as a substitute for religion--landscape and nature imbued with spirituality. Absorbed in the contemplation of nature, the spectator embarks on an unspoken dialogue with the landscape. The barriers of self drop, and we commune with what is around us, transcending ourselves in our unity with nature. We achieve an equipoise of self and surroundings.

Inspired by the Transcendentalists, our own task then might be to search out and uncover the hidden manifestations of the sublime in the world around us. For example, I approach the tree down the block, which stands mute and ignored, but which has a symmetry, a majesty, a beauty pulsating with life striving towards the sky. It is not enough for me just to see this tree. I must go further and study it, understand the ecology and taxonomy, explore its role in the biome, and then with this understanding, describe it in words for oneself and others.

Emerson believed in a verbal responsibility and mission: "Expressing our thoughts and feelings is not only one of the fundamental aspects of human nature ... but also one of the main purposes of human life." The writer's highest role is to be a poet, a conveyor of truth translated to meaning and more heightened emotion. Poetry is in the world, in people and things, and it is the poet's job to catch it and write it down. For Emerson, the poetry of the outdoors is the intentional and artful description of aesthetics and meaning. The poet can serve as a "guide" where words can emancipate and liberate.

With Emerson, we thus get a poetical, epigrammatical literary style that serves as a kind of scripture. Indeed much of his writing was designed for oratory, and the bulk of his income came from speaking tours. There is both an intellectual and emotional satisfaction in the linearity of Emerson's logic—from a celebration of individual freedom to the responsibility to seek out and understand both the beauty and facts of nature and, in the end, to strive and achieve transcendence and a personal sense of one's god. Not religion, not politics, not even past philosophy, but rather nature was a point of departure for Emerson regarding how to live most appropriately. Nature was his muse, and it is not surprising that Emerson gained fame for his poetry too, leveraging the form to communicate a natural aesthetic and genuine feeling. In his poem "Each and All," Emerson reflects on this profound connection:

> *Over me soared the eternal sky,*
> *Full of light and of deity;*
> *Again I saw, again I heard,*
> *The rolling river, the morning bird; —*
> *Beauty through my senses stole;*
> *I yielded myself to the perfect whole.*

ESSAI 46
Thoreau

*We can never have enough of nature. We must be
refreshed by the sight of inexhaustible vigor.... We
need to witness our own limits transgressed....*

—*Henry David Thoreau*

On a recent spring day, when the temperature rose into the
70s, I strung up a hammock in my side yard alongside our
stream under the shade of overhanging trees. I read for a bit,
and then, a bit bored, I decided to try to notice the world
around me. Although I've always had a fascination with larger
natural elements—the geology of the land or the towering
maples, beeches, and oaks—I decided to focus my attention
that day more on the wildlife nearby.

Here is what I saw during a 20-minute stretch: several
House Sparrows; many American Robins; an eastern gray
squirrel; a Mourning Dove; a delightfully yellow American
Goldfinch (the state bird of New Jersey); a sedate eastern
cottontail rabbit; a scrabbling eastern chipmunk; a pair of Blue
Jays and the nest they were building; hovering bumblebees; and
a Common Grackle. (These wildlife sightings do not include
my teen children sunning nearby, nor the gallivanting of my
golden retriever.)

I found the act of noticing nature, identifying species and

type, and then recording what I saw, deeply satisfying. I simultaneously felt part of the world around me while able to stand back and appreciate it. I had been reading excerpts from the journals of Henry David Thoreau, and he was a role model for this type of natural immersion and study. While Ralph Waldo Emerson created the gospel of Transcendentalism, Henry David Thoreau made it more visceral, acting out its tenets as a peripatetic prophet of the world around us. In his writing, Thoreau immerses us in the detail and grandeur of nature, recounting his excursions and what he found out in the world while providing his spiritual take. His writing is an inspiration to thoughtfulness and a goad to natural immersion.

Thoreau's journey essays—"Ktaadin" (1848) and "A Week on the Concord and Merrimack Rivers" (1849)—establish early on his view of nature as something critical to the development of the individual. In the Concord/Merrimack essay, he wrote, "I feel that I draw nearest to understanding the great secret of my life in my closest intercourse with nature … I suppose that what in other men is religion is in me love of nature." Thoreau advocates a personal relationship with the natural world where individuality and insight lead to a perception of immanence and growing spirituality. Nature for Thoreau was the big test, where the seemingly prosaic could become heroic and fulfilling.

In his most famous work, *Walden; or Life in the Woods*, Thoreau delineates a philosophy based on solitude, simplification, freedom, personal experience, self-confidence, responsibility, curiosity, local knowledge, and literary aspiration. Here are some quotes that I pulled from Walden to demonstrate these ethics:

> *I went to the woods because I wished to live deliberately, to front only the essential facts of life, and see if I could not learn what it had to teach, and not, when I came to die, discover that I had not lived.*

It is never too late to give up our prejudices.

If I repent of anything, it is very likely to be my good behavior....

Most of the luxuries, and many of the so-called comforts of life, are not only not dispensable, but positive hindrances to the elevation of mankind.

I have been anxious to improve the nick of time ... to stand on the meeting of two eternities, the past and future, which is precisely the present moment; to toe that line....

I was the self-appointed inspector of snow-storms and rain-storms, and did my duty faithfully; surveyor ... of forest paths and all across-lot routes.

I would rather sit in the open air, for no dust gathers on the grass.... I would rather sit on a pumpkin and have it all to myself than be crowded on a velvet cushion.

We need the tonic of wildness—to wade sometimes in the marshes where the bittern and meadow-hen lurk, and hear the boomings of the snipe; to smell the whispering sedge where only some wilder and more solitary fowl builds her nest, and the mink crawls with its belly close to the ground.

At the same time that we are earnest to explore and learn all things, we require that all things be mysterious and unexplorable, that land and sea be infinitely wild, unsurveyed and unfathomed by us because unfathomable.

God himself culminates in the present moment ... we are enabled to apprehend all what is sublime and noble only by the perpetual instilling and drenching of the reality which surrounds us.

I wanted to live deep and suck out all the marrow of life.

Thoreau lived in his small, self-built shack in the woods near Walden Pond for just two years. Before that and afterward, he lived in Concord, maintaining a daily ritual that consisted of writing in the morning and taking long walks of three to four hours in the afternoon. Inspired by Emerson, Thoreau kept a daily journal where he captured both the details of the natural world that he saw on his walks and the meaning that adhered to them. The journals capture seasons, sunsets, rivers, elms, orchards, old roads, views from heights, sunrises, flowers, willows, woodlots, and old farms. There are evocative descriptions where Thoreau serves as a highly-present, imperative narrator, urging us to see the world with him and to take away a heightened awareness.

Thoreau called his walks "saunters" drawing on the origin of the word from the pilgrim journeys in France to holy places, and for Thoreau, his walks were indeed a search for something sacred. The holy land in which he walked was within 10 or so miles of the town of Concord, and Thoreau treasured the depth with which he could explore and understand his small region, celebrating hyper-locality as better than traveling abroad.

Thoreau had a psychological and ecological commitment to Concord and its environs; it came alive in his writing as a source of metaphor and inspiration to transcendence. Thoreau went out into the landscape to search for and develop his own character, looking not to tomes of the Enlightenment or classical antiquity, but to the local elm nearby as a source of learning and strength. He believed in Emerson's construct: "Particular natural facts are symbols of particular spiritual facts." Thoreau used his journal writing to transmute the facts and feelings of his walks into his inspiration. For him, it was an ethical endeavor.

Below I have curated quotes from Thoreau's journal as a

guide to perhaps a broader set of thinking as we explore the world around us in our own ecological-literary practice:

I have met with but one or two persons in the course of my life who understood the art of taking walks daily—...to positively exercise both body and spirit, and to succeed to the highest and worthiest ends by the abandonment of all specific ends—who had a genius for sauntering.

...this word "saunter" ...is happily derived from 'idle people who roved about the country [in medieval times]...under the pretense of going a'la Sainte Terre,' to the Holy Land.

Pursue some path, however narrow and crooked, in which you can walk with love and reverence. Wherever a man separates from the multitude and goes his own way, there is a fork in the road....

The mass of mankind who live in houses of shops, or are bent upon their labor ... know nothing of the beautiful days which are passing about and around them. Is not such a day worthy of a hymn?

I set out once more to climb the mountain of the earth, for my steps are symbolic steps, and in all my walking I have not reached the top of the earth yet.

As I come over the hill, I hear the wood thrush singing his evening lay. This is the only bird whose note affects me like music, affects the flow and tenor of my thought, my fancy and imagination. It lifts and exhilarates me. It is inspiring. It is a medicative draught to my soul.

And then for my afternoon walks, I have a garden, larger than any artificial garden that I have read of and far more attractive to me....

Man's eye...demands the sober colors of the earth for its daily diet.

Concord is the oldest inland town in New England, perhaps in the States, and the walker is peculiarly favored here.

I have been nailed down to this my native region so long and steadily, and made to study and love this spot of earth more and more.

I can easily walk ten, fifteen, twenty any number of miles, commencing at my own door, without going by any house, without crossing a road except where the fox and mink do.

It matters not where or how far you travel ... but how much alive you are.

The poet has made the best roots in his native soil of any man, and is the hardest to transplant. The man who is often thinking that it is better to be somewhere else than where he is excommunicates himself. If a man is rich and strong anywhere, it must be on his native soil.

I want nothing new if I can but have a tithe of the old secured to me.

A man dwells in his native valley like a corolla in its calyx, like an acorn in its cup. Here, of course, is all that you love, all that you expect, all that you are.

Now I yearn for one of those old, meandering, dry, uninhabited roads, which lead away from towns, which lead us away from temptation, which conduct to the outside of the earth ... along which you may travel like a pilgrim, going no-whither ... where your spirit is free ... where your head is more in heaven than your feet are on earth.... There I can walk and recover the lost child that I am....

A vista.... The prospect of a vast horizon must be accessible in our neighborhood. Where men of enlarged views may be educated. An unchangeable kind of wealth, a real estate.

The scenery, when it is truly seen, reacts on the life of the seer. How to live. How to get the most of life.

I am accustomed to regard the smallest brook with as much interest for the time being as if it were the Orinoco or Mississippi.

What art can surpass the rows of maples and elms and swamp white oaks—...in variety and gracefulness—conforming to the curves of the river.

What are these rivers and hills, these hieroglyphics which my eyes behold?

Be not preoccupied with looking. Go not to the object; let it come to you. ... What I need is not to look at all, but a true sauntering of the eye.

I rest and take my lunch on Lee's Cliff, looking toward Baker Farm. What is a New England landscape this sunny August day? A weather-painted house and barn, with an orchard by its side, in midst of a sandy field surrounded by green woods, with a small blue lake on one side.

Our town has lost some of its venerableness. No longer will our eyes rest on [the elm's] massive gray trunk, like a vast Corinthian column by the wayside; no longer shall we walk in its lofty, spreading dome.

The grass so short and fresh, the tender yellowish-green and silvery foliage of the deciduous trees lighting up the landscape, the birds now most musical, the sorrel beginning to redden the fields with ruddy health,—all these things make earth now a paradise.

There is no such thing as pure objective observation. Your observation, to be interesting, i.e. to be significant, must be subjective.

There is just as much beauty visible to us in the landscape as we are prepared to appreciate.

He is the richest who has the most use for nature as raw material of tropes and symbols with which to describe his life. ... If I am overflowing with life, am rich in experience for which I lack expression, then nature will be my language full of poetry....

I desire to speak somewhere without bounds, in order that I may attain to an expression in some degree adequate to the truth of which I have been convinced.

It is as a leaf which hangs over my head in the path. I bend the twig and write my prayers on it; then letting it go, the bow springs up and shows the scrawl to heaven.

Write often, write upon a thousand themes, rather than long at a time, not trying to turn too many feeble [somesaults] in the air ... Antaeus-like be not long absent from the ground.

Nature gets thumbed like an old spelling book.

I succeed best when I recur to my experience not too late, but within a day or two; when there is some distance, but enough freshness.

...it is the marriage of the soul with nature that makes the intellect fruitful, that gives birth to the imagination.

You must live in the present, launch yourself on every wave, find your eternity in each moment.

I love Nature partly because she is not a man, but a retreat from him. None of his institutions control or pervade her. In her midst I can be glad with an entire gladness.

Sympathy with nature is evidence of perfect health. You cannot perceive beauty but with a serene mind.

Every natural form—palm leaves and acorns, oak leaf and sumach and dodder—are untranslatable aphorisms.

With our senses applied to the surrounding world we are reading our own physical and corresponding moral revolutions.

I think that the existence of man in nature is the divinest and most startling of all facts.

Give me the obscure life, the cottage of the poor and humble, the workdays of the world, the barren fields, the smallest share of things, but poetic perception

I sympathize with weeds perhaps more than with the crop they choke, they express so much vigor. They are the truer crop which the earth more willingly bears.

A roseate redness, clear as amber, suffuses the low western sky about the sun, in which the small clouds are mostly melted, only their golden edges still revealed. The atmosphere there is like some kind of wine, perchance, or molten cinnabar, if that is red, in which also all kinds of pearls and precious stones are melted.

It is enough that I please myself with my writing; I am then sure of an audience.

ESSAI 47
Whitman (Part One)

I am the poet of commonsense and of the demonstrable and of immortality.

—*Walt Whitman*

Walt Whitman was born on Long Island (as was I), grew up in the West Hills area (I did too), spent his young adult years in New York (same with me), and finished his life in New Jersey (as I am doing presently). His experience and what he writes about resonates personally and universally.

Whitman's poetry confronts us—what if we've lived our lives in entirely the wrong way, doing the wrong things, worrying and striving towards the wrong objectives, and not seeing or understanding what is truly important? In his 1855 poem "Song of Myself" Whitman writes, "I loafe and invite my soul, I lean and loafe at my ease ... observing a spear of summer grass." Here Whitman surreptitiously invites us to assume a different posture in the world, one where we stop hurrying, open ourselves to contemplation, ease our minds, and observe the simplest things. He creates an urgency, an imperative almost, to assume an attitude inclined to a more accurate sense of the world.

Whitman possessed both the heights of arrogance and the depths of humility. He starts "Song of Myself" boldly—"I

CELEBRATE myself." He asserts, "I am the poet of common sense and of demonstrable immortality." "I too am not a bit tamed, I too am untranslatable, I sound my barbaric yawp over the roofs of the world." "I exist as I am, that is enough...." Whitman captures the fact that although he is a common everyday sort, in his commonality, he has an ultimate role to play, a purpose to explicate nature, the world, and the universe, evoking its wild nativity.

First and foremost, Whitman is a teacher: "What I assume you shall assume." He promises us that his poetry will, "... follow you whoever you are from the present hour, my words itch at your ears till you understand them." "What is known I strip away ... I launch all men forward with me into the unknown." "I am not to be denied ... I compel ... I have stores plenty and to spare ... You can do nothing and be nothing but what I will infold you." Whitman is authoritative in his tone, seeking not to proscribe but to leverage poetry as a future-forward goad to the reader. He writes:

I tramp a perpetual journey.

My signs are a rain-proof coat and good shoes and a staff cut from the woods;...

I have no chair, nor church nor philosophy;

I lead no man to a dinner-table or library or exchange,

But each man and each woman of you I lead upon a knoll,

My left hand hooks you round the waist,

My right hand points to landscapes of continents, and a plain public road.

Not I, not any one else can travel that road for you,

You must travel it yourself.

Just as Henry David Thoreau calls out that "the mass of men lead lives of quiet desperation" (prescribing in Walden a life of simplicity, proximity to nature, and attendance to daily life), Walt Whitman hopes to act as a guide displaying the reality of the world for us to travel. Whitman writes, "Long enough you have dreamed contemptible dreams, Now I wash the gum from your eyes, You must habit yourself to the dazzle of the light, and of every moment of your life."

This is indeed a call to action, but what exactly is he asking us to see? First, Whitman implores us to stop judging people, objects, or our surroundings. In "Song of Myself" we see long lists of professions, doings, circumstances, geography, animals, and plants. In the preface, he notes, "Each precise object or condition or combination or process exhibits a beauty." He highlights ordinary people in their most prosaic activities with exhaustive detail and sympathy. His lists are a frenetic compilation of nouns, subjects, and objects, composed in the vernacular of New York in the mid-19th century. We hear of the pure contralto singing in the organ loft, the carpenter dressing his plank, the children riding home for Thanksgiving dinner, the pilot heaving the kingpin, the mate in the whaleboat, the duck shooter, the deacons at altar, the spinning-girl at her wheel, the farmer with oats and rye, the lunatic carried to an asylum, the jour printer, the anatomist with malformed limbs on the table, the quadroon girl sold as a slave, the drunkard by the barroom stove, the machinist, the gate-keeper, the policeman on his beat, the marksman at the turkey-shoot, new immigrants on a wharf, dancing youths, an overseer in his saddle, a trapper on a Michigan creek, the reformer on a platform, the squaw selling moccasins, the connoisseur at the gallery, deckhands on a steamboat, two sisters at the loom, a new mother, the Yankee girl in the mill, the woman in labor, the paving man, the reporter, the sign-painter, the conductor of the band, the canal-boy on the towpath, the bookkeeper at his desk, the shoemaker waxing thread, the lady sitting for a daguerrotype, the drover watching his drove, the peddler with his pack, the bride in a rumpled white dress, the prostitute in a shawl, the President with his secretaries, matrons on the piazza, the crew loading a fish-smack, the tinners, the masons, seasons pursuing each other, the Fourth of July, a ploughing plougher, a mowing mower, the stump standing thick and round, the torches shining in the dark on the Chattahoochee, the sleeping city, and the sleeping country, etc.

With such a list, on and on and never really complete, Whitman gives us a metonymy of life and meaning, asking us to exist in celebration of people and actions and the world around us. "The whirling and whirling is elemental in me." Whitman promotes a democracy of meaning—that in the seeming unremarkable, we must notice and remark on all. In the ordinary one can find sustenance, beauty, and even divinity.

ESSAI 48
Whitman (Part Two)

Whitman's ultimate metonym is the "leaf of grass." In "Song of Myself," he cites the leaf as a symbol of simplicity and phenomenological intent, and as a metaphor for the pages of his book. Whitman suggests that the simplest things can encompass much larger meaning: "a leaf of grass is no less than the journeywork of the stars." The leaf has none of the seeming grandeur of a stately tree, nor the surface aesthetic of a blooming rose bush but is worthy of our study nonetheless. It represents one of the smallest natural flora, just one of many leaves in a larger lawn. It is thus humble and seemingly uninteresting, but Whitman celebrates this humility and sameness: "I guess it must be the flag of my disposition, out of hopeful green stuff woven; Or I guess it is the handkerchief of the lord."

Whitman christens this smallest thing with the highest divinity: "The smallest sprout shows there is really no death." The poet must loaf on a lawn and contemplate the meaning of the grassy leaves, a meaning which ranges from the factual detail of the single leaf to the infinity and immortality that the leaf implies. The explication of the leaf is then translated through poetry. Whitman urges us not to see his writing, i.e., his book *Leaves of Grass*, as concrete or manufactured. The book's pages are not paper glued together and bound, but a sheaf of leaves, a floral emanation emitted by nature and then gathered up by the poet. With its ranging free-verse, the poetry eschews literary form and becomes living flow sans structure or restriction.

Whitman emphasizes, "A morning glory at my window satisfies me more than the metaphysics of books." Whitman wants us to experience the world firsthand by getting outside, asking us to join him in the "open air." "If you would understand me go to the heights or water-shore." "No shutter'd room or school can commune with me." The poetry goads us to do primary research in nature, not relying on old writers and given wisdom: "You shall no longer take things at second or third hand ... nor look through the eyes of the dead ... nor feed on the specters in books." Focusing on the most prosaic, he writes, "Oxen that rattle the yoke or halt in the shade, what is it that you express in your eyes? It seems to me more than all the print I have read in my life." Observation of fauna, flora, and people, is the path to spirituality: "...every motion and every spear of grass and the frames and spirits of men and women and all that concerns them are unspeakably perfect miracles all referring to all and each distinct in its place."

Whitman saw the miraculous as emanating from the concrete world in which he walked and in what he observed. He did not believe in a god distinct from people and nature. He departed radically from the Judeo-Christian ethic where God is seen as a separate, higher entity. For Whitman, there was no distinction between God and the world. Human uniqueness and actions, and the facets of objects and nature, sum up to the divine: "Why should I wish to see God better than this day? I see something of God each hour of the twenty-four, and each moment then, In the faces of men and women I see God, and in my own face in the glass; I find letters from God [leaves] dropped in the street, and every one is signed by God's name." God is both everywhere and in each thing: "...and there is not object so soft but it makes for a hub for the wheeled universe."

Whitman calls on us to see divinity first and foremost as instantaneous. "You must habit yourself to the dazzle of the light and of every moment of your life." "There was never any more inception than there is now, nor any more youth or age than there is now; and will never be any more perfection than there is now, nor any more heaven or hell than there is now." In this immediacy, one realizes perfection, eternity, and immortality. He writes in the poem "To Think of Time," "How beautiful are the animals! How perfect is my soul! How perfect the earth and the minutest things upon it! ... I swear now that everything has an eternal soul! I swear I think there is nothing but immortality!"

Whitman shines a celestial headlamp on what there is to be seen: "...the judges judge but as the sun falling around a helpless thing"-- and then shares what he finds with us. The poet's verses "...are hymns in the praise of things." In his other poems, we hear these hymns. In "Crossing Brooklyn Ferry," Whitman views the river shore seeing: "The glories strung like beads on my smallest sights and hearings, on the walk in the street and the passage over the river ... You furnish your parts towards eternity, Great or small, you furnish your parts toward the soul." Here we see how the landscape becomes not just fodder for poetic inspiration, but poetry itself. In his poem "Manahatta," Whitman offers us, "A million people—manners free and superb—open voices—hospitality.... City of hurried and sparkling waters! City of spires and masts! City nested in bays! My city!"

In both poems, we see landscape first as history and place (Manahatta was the original native American name of Manhattan), then as visual aesthetic rising to art, and then further as spiritual and immanent. The land around us becomes a great Whitman-esque free-verse poem filled with complexity, beauty, and the miraculous. And if we take up the charge, we

too can become the poet, following in Whitman's steps—
picaresque and peripatetic, virtuous and vigorous, soulful and
sun-filled. Our journeys are the poem, our turns in the road
the stanzas, and our feet the rhythm of the verse. "The known
universe has one complete lover and that is the greatest poet."

ESSAI 49
Orogeny

There was wide wand'ring for the greediest eye,
To peer about upon variety;
Far round the horizon's crystal air to skim,
And trace the dwindled edgings of its brim;
To picture out the quaint, and curious bending
Of a fresh woodland alley, never ending;
Or by the bowery clefts, and leafy shelves,
Guess were the jaunty streams refresh themselves.
I gazed awhile, and felt as light, and free
As though the fanning wings of Mercury
Had played upon my heels: I was light-hearted,
And many pleasures to my vision started;

   — John Keats, "I stood tip-toe upon a little hill"

There is always that pause when one first stands at a summit—a caesura at the top of a hill or mountain, the roof of a building, or the peak of a church. At that moment, one takes in the sweep of the surrounding land, surveying it from above, an untethered view, god-like in aspect, and lifted in feeling.

In my travels, I have searched out peaks as both physical achievement and just to see what's what. Two summers ago, I traveled to Portugal, where my wife and I eschewed the tourist bus to climb our way up to the Castle of the Moors in Sintra outside of Lisbon. We scrambled over battlements and through the old gardens, taking in the view north and east, and then south and west. I've also been to the tops of mountains in Colorado on ski trips, bundled up in layers of clothes and perched on the verge of steep slopes, 11,000 feet above sea level with a broad mountain-scape miles around, fearful of the upcoming plunge. I've been to St. Paul's Cathedral, where in the basement, one can see the tomb of the naval hero Horatio Nelson and then wind one's way up through nave and dome to get a broad view atop central London in her varied historical glory. In South Africa near Cape Town on the flat summit of Table Mountain, one is high enough up to espy both the Atlantic Ocean and the Indian Ocean on either side of the African continent. And, in my hometown of Ridgewood, New Jersey, on the evening of 9/11/2001, we made our way to the eponymous ridge where a clear view of the city could be had with the smoke still rising from the fallen towers.

As part of a business trip once, I took a helicopter ride from Las Vegas south towards the Grand Canyon. We took off from McCarran airport and flew from the strip behind us towards the ridge of mountains that separates the Las Vegas basin from Lake Meade. Las Vegas is located in a 600-square mile valley, surrounded on all sides by mountains. On the rare rainy days, there is the risk of floods, and on that day, the human-made and natural gullies were flowing with water, and the skies were still overcast from morning showers. With the glitz of the strip behind us, we approached the ridge catching a view of old WWII magnesium mines. Back in the 1930s, the Nevada senator Patrick McCarran, for whom the airport was named, convinced President Franklin Roosevelt to fund a magnesium mining company. By World War II, the mines were supply magnesium for munitions exploding around the world.

We crested the ridge and received a view of the massive

Hoover Dam with the turquoise spread of Lake Meade curving behind it. As a kid I had read the Zane Grey novel, Boulder Dam (an earlier name for Hoover Dam). It was a Bildungsroman about a washed-up college football star in the early 1930s working different parts of the dam during its construction, overcoming physical and emotional challenges while also foiling a plot to blow the dam up. Hoover Dam was huge below; the helicopter pilot told me that it used enough concrete to build a 3,000-mile highway.

The last part of the trip entailed a short flight up the Grand Canyon. We flew beneath the rim, yet the canyon floor was still 4,000 feet below, with the Colorado River's muddy ribbon winding its corrosive way through ridges and rocks beneath. The distance to the canyon sides and down to the floor was hard to measure and discomfiting. From the helicopter, the monumental seemed minuscule. The giant hotels of the Las Vegas strip, magnesium mines, Hoover Dam, Lake Meade, the mighty Colorado River all seemed toy-like with less significance. The heights minimized importance, unbalancing one's perspective, and humbling us as well. As the seemingly giant things recede from on high, our surety follows suit.

A decade ago, I attended the Superbowl at the newly built AT&T Stadium in Dallas, Texas. In Texas, everything is bigger, and that is especially true of the stadium. It seats 105,000 people and boasts a 160-by-72 foot high-definition scoreboard/ TV screen. I was seated high up, so I had the choice between watching the game bird's-eye, tiny action figures below, or more easily on the big screen in front of me.

The next morning I drove with a friend to northwestern Arkansas for a business meeting. We took off on the six-hour drive from Dallas heading northeast through the flatness of Texas, crossing the Red River into plains country in Oklahoma, hitting I-40, and turning east. I-40 took us to Fort Smith perhaps best known as the primary western terminus for the infamous "Trail of Tears," which was not just one trail but a group of routes from Georgia, Alabama, and Tennessee that the Choctaw and Cherokee people traversed as part of their forced migration to eastern Oklahoma in the 1830s. Turning north on I-540, we crossed the Arkansas River and entered the Ozarks.

The Ozarks are a hilly region encompassing southern Missouri, northwestern Arkansas, and eastern Oklahoma. The Ozarks, along with the Ouachita Mountains (south of the Arkansas River) comprise the "U.S. Interior Highland Region," the only significant highland area between the Appalachians east and the Rockies out west. More of a plateau than actual mountains, the Ozarks are rolling hill country with a higher, mountainous area in the south called the Boston Mountains. Driving up from the south, we cut through this higher area, which in parts reminded me of the New York Catskills near my home. Near Fayetteville, home of the University of Arkansas, the land became more typical of most of the Ozarks. We enjoyed the rolling Ozark hills for the last hour of our drive—the highway roller-coastering up and down and around curves.

The Ozarks are the eroded remains of Paleozoic islands and surrounding reefs from a sea that existed a few hundred million geologic years ago. Limestone and sedimentary rock underlies the Ozarks, testifying to aquatic origins in the distant past. This ancient remnant of past beaches, lagoons and seas sit as a cynosure in the middle of our country--an upland escarpment on the verge of the vast plains. The Ozarks have emerged as both a booming business and tourist area. The Walmart Corporation's headquarters sits in hilly Bentonville, while further north, vacationers enjoy the Lake of the Ozarks in Missouri. People now flock to these mountains, paving roads through the valleys and topping the hills with new homes.

They move upward to the heights, divining and devising their destiny.

The Taconic mountain range stretches from the lower New York State Hudson Highland area, east across the Hudson River, up the border of New York and Connecticut, into Massachusetts, where they include the Berkshire Mountains, and then into Vermont where they are called the Green Mountains. The name "Taconic" itself derives from native Algonquin, spelled alternatively "taghkanic," meaning "in the trees."

Driving through these hills and trees, the romantic quaintness of landscape strikes one. Three hundred-year-old villages with their original inns and federal homes are spotted every few miles. Revolutionary armies marched close by, with Ethan Allen's Green Mountain Boys invading New York State, followed by Henry Knox dragging 60 tons of cannon over the mountain range to the siege of Boston, forcing the British to abandon the city. In spring, the streams and rivers roar over rocks and waterfalls. In summer, the lakes and parks fill with campers. The fall foliage invites an annual pilgrimage from New York or Boston. And, in winter, as James Taylor sang, "the Berkshires seem dreamlike on account of that frosting."

The mountains are ancient. The Taconics are the oldest mountain range in North America and one of the world's oldest. Four hundred sixty million years ago, an island chain the size of present-day Japan overrode the eastern edge of the proto-North American tectonic plate creating an orogeny, a mountain-building geologic event. The edge of the continental plate folded and pushed upwards, forming a chain of mountains. The original Taconic mountains were much more extensive than now--Himalayan in size--but have been worn down by erosion to heights ranging from 2,000 to 3,800 feet. Two subsequent orogenies, the more northern Acadian and the more southern Alleghanian, both further west than the Taconic ridge, created the bulk of what we know today as the Appalachian mountain chain. We can see the orogenic folds of the Taconics today, as the rock strata throughout the chain poke up angled, jumbled, and buckled. The staccato of the name "Taconic" matches the spiky nature of the land.

I have hiked in the Taconic range in New Hampshire, Vermont, New York, and New Jersey. Glaciers have worked their magic: fissuring the granite, tumbling and strewing boulders, and shaving off peaks. Native trees cover the hills—oak and maple and pine—secondary and sometimes tertiary growth now grown large on their own.

We travel from the urbs and suburbs to these mountains to find something about the land, but also for the view to see something larger than what our river-valley, ground-level existence can supply. Perhaps we are looking for a personal orogeny. Maybe we hope for an upthrusting of the soul, reaching for the spiritual heights driven by tectonic forces of our being. We climb to castle battlements, to the tops of churches, to the pinnacles of skyscrapers, and to mountain peaks in search of perspective and gleanings of meaning. On Olympus, perhaps the ephemeral becomes immanent.

ESSAI 50
Books

In nature's infinite book of secrecy
A little I can read.

— *William Shakespeare*

I thought I might provide an admittedly self-indulgent bibliographic essay to perhaps inspire further reading into topics around nature, landscape, philosophy, and ecology. You might get a sense of my literary Bildungsroman here, which might unfortunately come across as egotistical or annoying (apologies if so). You also might get a sense of how reading and research can create a web of understanding and, notwithstanding any of the titles below, be inspired to explore subjects to your own taste.

First and foremost, the idea of the "Essai" came from my reading of Michel De Montaigne's own *Essais*. Montaigne wrote primarily from his Bordeaux castle retirement in the 1570s and 1580s. His writings not only created a new literary form, the personal essay, but his works also evoke a sense of curiosity, honesty, and humanism as a touchstone of a life well-lived. The *Essais* themselves are accessible in Donald Frame's translation and can be read in short chunks. Reading them provides lessons in the classics—Montaigne does not hesitate to quote favorites like Horace, Lucretius, etc.—as applied to everyday life. In his essai, "Of Solitude," he writes with wisdom: "...be content with yourself ... to fix it on definite and limited thoughts in which it may take pleasure: and, after understanding the true blessings ... to rest content with them, without any desire to prolong life or reputation." In addition to the *Essais* themselves, Sarah Bakewell's *How to Live, or A Life of Montaigne*, provides an excellent biography of Montaigne and his philosophy, such as it is.

Emerson and Thoreau›s essays and writings are critical to understanding the spiritual impetus and idealism behind our conceptions of nature in the United States today. Emerson's essays "Self-Reliance," "The American Scholar," and "Nature" are simultaneously epigrammatic and tough to wade through. The biographer Robert Richardson's *Emerson: Mind on Fire* is accessible and beautifully wrought, providing the intellectual underpinnings of Emerson's thinking as well as the context of his times. For Thoreau, in addition to formal works like *Walden*, *Walking*, and his journey essays, I also read a compendium his nature writing culled from his daily journals: *Henry David Thoreau: An American Landscape*, compiled by Robert Rothwell. More recently, John Kaag's *American Philosophy* fleshes out the impact of the American Romantic movement on today's sensibilities.

Further philosophical inquiry led me to the popular works of Will Durant, including both his *Story of Philosophy* and select reading from his multi-volume *The Story of Civilization*, co-written with Ariel Durant. This led to a variety of primary homework, including Rousseau (*Reveries of the Solitary Walker*) and Spinoza (excerpts from *Ethics*), as well as William James and Jean Paul Sartre. Anthony Kronman's 1,076-page *Confessions of a Born Again Pagan* remains just 25% read by me. His threading the needle between philosophy, scientific rationalism, and a broader religiosity is both admirable and ecumenical. Most of this reading informed my sensibility about man's role and place in nature, reinforcing my belief in humility before immanence.

My belief in the inspiring power of nature myths, came not surprisingly from Joseph Campbell's *Hero with a Thousand Faces* as well as my long-ago reading of the classic *Bullfinch's Mythology* as a teen. It is the shortest of literary steps from these sources to my love of the Tolkien oeuvre, which captures the tale of heroic journey and drama across a broad landscape. It is then just another short step to historical fiction such as Kenneth Robert's *Northwest Passage*, where we read the tale of Robert's Rangers foray up Lake Champlain to Canada and back down the Connecticut River during the French and Indian War of the 1750s, or Tolstoy's epic of the Napoleonic wars, *War and Peace*, where Pierre Bezukhov quixotically ventures out to the central artillery emplacement at the Battle of Borodino, or Michael Shaara's *Killer Angels* where Colonel Joshua Chamberlain girds his Maine regiment to hold the end of the union line at Gettysburg, or Mark Helprin's *A Soldier of the Great War* where young Alessandro Giuliani survives the Tyrol front of northern Italy in World War I. The combination of both grand strategic scope, battle tactics, and individual soldier experience can be found from great historical writers: Bruce Catton, Douglass Freeman, Shelby Foote, Barbara Tuchman, William Manchester, John Keegan, and David Hackett Fischer (among many others).

The relevance of landscape and landscape history began for me in college, when I took Ruben Rainey's course in American landscape history at the University of Virginia followed later by Kathryn Gleason's graduate-level global landscape history survey at the University of Pennsylvania. Depth of knowledge around historical landscape forms came from William Cronon's *Changes in the Land*, John Stilgoe's *Common Landscape of America* and *Borderland*, and especially Christopher Alexander's

A Pattern Language. Alexander, especially captures the idea that curiosity and analysis are required to understand, appreciate, and enjoy the land and ensure utility.

The fascination with geology, as evidenced by topography, came from the writings of John McPhee. His *Annals of the Former World*, compiles five previous books where he traced the tectonic history of North America using the route of I-80 as a cartographical MacGuffin. There is a booming literary genre around trees and their ecological importance, but if there is one arboreal book to read, it is Richard Power's novel *The Overstory* about the epic mid-20th century battle to save trees from disease and logging.

Many articles and books can bolster ecology and environmental awareness, but I often find them tendentious and overwrought. There are a select few must-reads. Barbara Novak's *Nature and Culture* grounds us in what nature (and religion) meant to the first generation of American landscape artists in the 1800s and gives us an overview of past conceptions of nature, wilderness, and garden. In the 20th century, the artist and illustrator Eric Sloane bemoaned the disappearing values of 19th-century agricultural life in words and pictures celebrating elements of nature, artisanal crafts and traditions, and building forms in books like *America Yesterday* and *Our Vanishing Landscape*. Douglas Tallamy's *Nature's Best Hope* prescribes what we can do today to help succor our immediate surroundings (i.e., our backyards) amid climate change. First-person lyrical accounts such as the works of Wendell Berry, Barry Lopez, and Aldo Leopold inform a reverence and humility confronting nature. Individual narratives like David Miller's *Awol on the Appalachian Trail* or Nathaniel Philbrick's *Second Wind* provide narratives of personal persistence confronting nature. Similarly, we can turn to the first-person vigor of the great poets: Keats and Wordsworth; Dickinson and Whitman; Frost and Oliver.

Across all of this, I recommend the dilettante's attitude—avoid over commitment, browse, and just enjoy what you enjoy.

I will end with our own neighborhoods. To find out about our own village, town, or county, we first walk around with curiosity. Then we can go to the local library where description and history abound for deeper understanding. Local historians love to tell stories and can provide the skinny on why things are the way they are in the local landscape. Knowing your home ground from the geology below to the topography above, from the flora to the fauna, and from the streets to the architecture alongside can be fascinating for some of us, but I think it's important for all. John Stilgoe writes, "Outside lies utterly ordinary space open to any casual explorer willing to find the extraordinary. Outside lies un-programmed awareness that at times becomes directed serendipity. Outside lies magic."

ESSAI 51
Transience

And what are these fluxions? The velocities of evanescent increments. And what are these same evanescent increments?

—George Berkeley

What is nature, but a dialectic of elements? Water erodes the land but then deposes sediment that rebuilds the land. Animals eat plants but then in death fertilize flora. Nature is interaction, micro and macro, across instants and eternities. The Greek philosopher Heraclitus wrote, "Everything changes, nothing stands still." Nothing is static in the universe, nor in the mind, nor in the soul. There is an impermanence to the world and within ourselves. "You could not step into the same river twice," Heraclitus writes, suggesting inherent transience even of things that seem permanent. Everything is in the act of becoming something else in every moment. Reality is dynamism.

"Plate Tectonics" is the now widely accepted geologic theory that the crust of the earth is comprised of interlocking plates that migrate over time, creating mountains, earthquakes, islands, cliffs, and valleys. The word tectonic originally meant something that pertained to building or constructing architectural forms. It is the idea of a force erecting something as small as a local bank building or as large as a continent's topology. The euphony of "tectonic" feels rigid and German-like (Teutonic) in attitude and intent. It has that abrupt onomatopoetic "ct" sound like rocks clinking, similar to words like enact, fact, erect, construct, detect, and concoct. We don't want our world's design to come from random whim, but from a theory of construction that adheres to logic. Tectonic steers us from the soft ethereal to the hard factual. We love tectonic explanations to rationalize the otherwise unimaginable scale of time, substances, and movement.

An escarpment is a geologic form that results from plate tectonics. An escarpment near my home—a high cliff that demarcates a broad valley below—came from volcanic magma pushing upward as the land was stretched apart due to the tectonic splitting of an old supercontinent a few hundred million years ago. An escarpment originally connoted a human-made mound fronting a rampart, with a steep outward facing slope and often with a ditch in front. Enemy forces would find it difficult to attack the escarpment. An escarpment is now more defined as a sharp cliff (aka a "scarp") from which the land around can be viewed.

Escarpment has that tilting "sc" digraph, which turns up in other similar words. To ascend to the top of an escarpment, one would have to scale it to scan the broad landscape. Think of a window-washing scaffold sticking out from the side of the building. A scalene triangle is one where the three sides are all unequal, and a cross-section of an escarpment would indeed be scalene as it is like a triangle on the verge of tipping over. We ascend the hill (soft s) and then reach the cliff (hard c). Scaling is the action we take to see the scene.

The escarpment's prominence is an estrangement from what is usual in the land; it is a scar on an otherwise smoother topography. An escarpment is harsh and cutting in its upthrust. The "sc" of escarpment also shares the discordant euphony of words like scathe, scorn, scar, scuffle, scare, scrap, scrape, scatter, scam, scorch, score, scrimp, scorpion, scratch, screech, scrawl, scoundrel, scum scavenge, sclerotic, scoff, scour, scourge, scurrilous, screw, scuttle, scythe, and scowl. There is something vertiginous about an escarpment; the scale of the view can often be scarifying. We climb up to see the world differently. We scan the land, not just viewing but intentionally looking, trying to scout what is going on. We can then descend and descant what we see, the good, and the not so good.

When we head down to the valley, we find a smoother, less harsh world. We see the bog, the fen, the swamp, the marsh— all monosyllabic evocations of wetlands. There is a restraint in the meaning of these words. We get bogged down in minutia. We become swamped by work. We can find ourselves in a personal quagmire, a morass of our own making. There is a mental image of boots stuck in the sucking mud—stinging mosquitoes, slithering reptiles, brambles, and thorns to fight through.

In 1728, William Byrd II led an expedition to map out the southern border of what was then the Virginia Colony. Near Norfolk, Virginia, there stretched a vast wetland, which Byrd named "The Great Dismal Swamp." From the view then of farmers and plantation owners, swamps were large, useless tracts of land. Indeed, since then, wetlands have either been something to drain and reclaim, or land deemed worthless, a dumping ground for trash and pollution. We now know the efficacy of marshes for the environment (e.g., the vast carbon capture of peat bogs), especially for wildlife. The Great Dismal Swamp is a significant stopover for birds on the Atlantic Flyway, the north/south route along the Atlantic coast for migrating species.

Another stop on the Atlantic Flyway is The Meadowlands in northern New Jersey near Manhattan. The Meadowlands are a vast stretch of grasslands surrounding the end of the Hackensack River as it flows into Newark Bay. Meadows are in-between landscapes. Stands of cedar originally covered the Meadowlands until Dutch farmers cleared the land for grass. Meadows are not truly cultivated farmland but are often harvested for hay. They are not marshes but are usually lower-lying and wetter than heath or prairie. They are landscapes in flux, from what might have once been cultivated farmland, transforming into an expanse of grass and wildflowers, and then perhaps evolving to woody shrubs and saplings and eventually to new woodlands. A meadow embodies the healthfulness of the land, with ground cover preventing erosion and providing screen for hedge animals. Meadow flowers delight the eye and provide pollen for bees. The medieval drink, "mead," shares the same Old English root as meadow, and mead comes from fermented honey from meadow pollen.

The nature writer Barry Lopez writes, "something emotive abides in the land." In our landscapes, we sense not just factually the sights or sounds or smells, but with a sixth sense of something more profound. From the escarp, we experience both a grandiosity of vision and a fear of the heights. From the marsh, we are in the midst of life's fullness but sometimes stuck and struggling through. Below the crag but above the bog, we can find the open field, the meadow where evolution of life is underway and which can serve as a metaphor for us. We are in a dialogue with our surroundings, a colloquy of curiosity as we listen to nature and put into words that which often defies definition. We seek the humility and awe of the natural world, capturing for ourselves the momentary equipoise before the inevitable evanescence.

ESSAI 52
Homeland

Where we love is home, home that our feet may leave, but not our hearts.

—*Oliver Wendell Holmes*

Central Park is an elongated rectangle, stretching in the south from 59th street in Manhattan's Midtown district up to 110th street in Harlem to the north. The park spans from Fifth Avenue westward to Central Park West (Eighth Avenue) from east to west. The park has 18,000 trees (comprising 200 species), multiple schist outcrops (schist is a gray metamorphic rock with shiny flecks of quartz and feldspar), 192 types of birds, 58 miles of walking paths, 7 different bodies of water (two ponds, a meer, a loch, a lake, a pool, a water, and a reservoir), hundreds of acres of lawns, meadows and woodlands, and about 9,000 park benches. For many New Yorkers, Central Park is their neighborhood, their backyard where they go daily or weekly to exercise, walk their dogs, or just sit and watch the goings-on.

You can make your way through Central Park using one of five different routing systems. The first consists of the many walking paths. These lead from entry gates most often downhill into the park, swooping under bridges, avoiding road crossings, circling open meadows, cutting through stands of woods, and navigating along lakes and ponds. Curvilinear walking in the park was meant to contrast with the surrounding city streets' grid geometry and offer an evolving view of new vistas as park-goers proceed forward. Topography and landscaping maximize the experience of nature, tranquility, and escape from the city through careful design. Walking was seen as the primary means of egress through the park.

The roadway "drives" represent a second system of movement through the park. There are four of them. The long East Drive and West Drive run south to north, up and down the park's right and left portions, respectively. The Terrace Drive connects the East Drive to the West Drive around 72nd street and borders the brick Bethesda Terrace that overlooks the central Lake. Finally, the Center Drive is the road along the southern and lower-east portions of the park. These drives all connect and form overlapping circuits. Originally intended for just horse carriage use, the Drives were later adapted for automobile traffic. Since mid-2018, all motor traffic has been prohibited, with the drives reserved now reserved just for bikers, runners, and pedestrians. The New York City Marathon route enters the upper park on the East Drive and ultimately finishes on the lower section of the West Drive each year.

A third pathway system is the four-mile-long Central Park Bridle Path for the commendably anachronistic few who still enjoy a good canter or trot. This path used to be longer but now is confined to circuits around the Onassis Reservoir and the North Meadow further up. I've walked the bridle path, and it has a more rural, less-developed, almost hidden feel than other ways through the park.

The fourth and arguably the most essential routing system for the park is a mostly unseen one. It consists of the four recessed transverse automobile roads that run crosstown at 66th, 79th, 86th, and 96th streets. The transverse roads are below the park's level, almost tunneling under the land, purposely hidden from the drives and the walking paths above. These roads allow city traffic to cross from east to west and west to east, without upsetting the serenity of the park goers.

Beyond these four types of roads and paths, one can, of course, take a fifth way through the park, which dispenses with formality. You can just cut across—climb over the fence, trek through the meadow, take an oblique angle. When I lived on the Upper East Side and walked to work in the western part of midtown, I used to do exactly this, using walking paths and roadways, but also cutting across meadows and through the woods.

Frederick Law Olmsted and Calvert Vaux created the original "Greensward" design for Central Park in 1857. Their plan had a dual intent. The first was democratic. The mass of city people had little access to nature: "The enjoyment of the choicest natural scenes in the country and the means of recreation connected with them is thus a monopoly, in a very peculiar manner, of a very few very rich people. The great mass of society, including those to whom it would be of the greatest benefit, is excluded from it." Olmsted's and Vaux's ambition with the park was to recreate the broad sense of nature available to the rich in their estate parks, capturing the variety of meadow, woodland, stream, and lake, as well as the careful placement of architecture within the land. You can see this populist theme with the naming of the entry gates into the park, which are not named for politicians or business people but with a more universal touch—Miner's Gate, Farmer's Gate, Women's Gate, Children's Gate, Scholar's Gate, Hunter's Gate, etc.

Olmsted further promulgated a psychological aesthetic: "If we analyze the operations of scenes of beauty upon the mind, and consider the intimate relation of the mind upon the nervous system and the whole physical economy, the action and reaction which constantly occur between bodily and mental conditions, the reinvigoration which results from such scenes is readily comprehended.... The enjoyment of scenery employs the mind without fatigue and yet exercises it; tranquilizes it and yet enlivens it; and thus, through the influence of the mind over the body gives the effect of refreshing rest and reinvigoration to the whole system." The physicality of the individual moving amidst the beauty of the scenery sustained body, mind, and even soul.

The design of Central Park looked to simultaneously capture a range of landscape ideals from the formality of French Classic parterres, to the English tradition of broad meadows and curvilinear paths, and then to a more elemental and wild American sublime. One sees this in the progression walking from the southeast entrance of the park at Grand Army Plaza, then strolling through the rectilinear Mall, stepping down to the Bethesda Terrace's classic architecture, circling the Lake and over the Bow Bridge, and then meandering into the wild Ramble. Whether one is looking to promenade on formal walkways, sit Wordsworth-like on a hill overlooking the Sheep Meadow, or get lost in the depths of the Ravine in the northern section of the park, there is a variety to the design to suit different needs and sensibilities.

Despite its European and classical tropes, Central Park's aesthetic has been become, over time and through repetition, peculiarly American. After initial success in park design, Olmsted founded his architecture firm which created other landscapes around the country, leveraging similar design elements to Central Park. I have come across his work (and those of his descendant company, Olmsted and Sons) in New Orleans's Audubon Park, Boston's Back Bay Fens, and Atlanta's Druid Hills. Close to where I live now is Goffle Brook Park, a long strip of designed landscape with the fields, paths, and meadows along a bubbling brook, designed by Olmsted and

Sons. The intermixing of formal approaches with lawns, thickets, terraces, and buildings has become a template not just for parks, but for college campuses, office complexes, and our own yards. The stately oak trees, expansive lawns, and brick-lined paths are aspirational designs to this day.

I have strong personal memories of Central Park, from races that I have run there, to relaxing outings with friends, to bike rides (and rollerblading back in the day). My time living in New York spanned the 1990s, and the memories of the park intertwine with meeting and dating my wife, followed by our first years of marriage. For 10 years, Central Park was my neighborhood and backyard. Like other places where I have lived, I view Central Park, and even Manhattan as a whole, as one of my "homelands"--places of emotional association, intimacy, knowledge, and memory. There are lands and places throughout our lives with which we have a deep affinity, and we gather and value these connections over time.

My first homeland was Long Island, where I lived from age 4 to 14, and where I biked and roamed with the freedom children still had in the 1970s. I've written about my hikes with my uncle and living unknowingly on a glacial moraine. There was the time when my brother and I rode our bikes from the hilly northern part of Long Island, where we lived, across to my grandparent's home in Massapequa Park on the flat glacial outwash plain of the South Shore. That bike ride, plus the summer visits to the beaches of Robert Moses State Park, my share-house in the Hamptons when I was in my 20s, and visits out to Montauk Point (where I proposed to my wife) all add to the affinity I have for my Long Island homeland.

Another homeland for me was the University of Virginia. I've always loved historic architecture and American history, and UVa had a surfeit of it. Moving soon after to Atlanta with its rolling hills, pine trees, and Civil War battle markers,

I became further immersed in the South. I remember when friends and I road in a pickup truck through western Georgia and southern Alabama to Panama City Beach, Florida. Most recently, my homeland has been Bergen County, New Jersey, with its historic Dutch farmhouse architecture, broad sandstone valleys, Victorian-era commuter towns, high ridges, and rolling hills.

I would argue that "homeland" ought to be a more elastic term. The land is not a summation of facts to know, but rather a canvass for our curiosity. It is something we simultaneously experience and remember, but also continue to seek. It is not something defined and set in stone, but rather evolves. Geographic definitions—town, county, state, nation—by their nature ignore the permeability of the people, lands, and the nature around us. There is an interconnectedness to our world that exceeds constructed delineations. I wonder whether the right conception of homeland should expand to be that of the Earth itself and that our commitment to our home needs to be a commitment to the larger natural world.

Perhaps we need a homeland heterodoxy. Land is not something to own, but something to steward. Land is not something to be sliced up, purchased, and controlled, but a place of participative cycles of nativity and devolution. Our sojourns across the land and the actions we take to sustain it are an acknowledgment not only of our current home, but also that the larger house needs constant care into the future. The philosopher Baruch Spinoza wrote, "In so far as the mind sees things in their eternal aspect, it participates in eternity." By seeking, understanding, and caring for our homelands, we are partaking in a larger contribution to the immanence of the world.

CPSIA information can be obtained
at www.ICGtesting.com
Printed in the USA
FSHW010723210121
77759FS

9 780578 802879